FIDEL CASTRO

A REVOLUTION CAN ONLY BE BORN FROM CULTURE AND IDEAS

Master lecture delivered by
H.E. Dr. Fidel Castro Ruz, President of the Republic of Cuba,
at the main lecture hall in the Central University
of Venezuela, on 3 February, 1999.

FOREWORD BY THE AUTHOR

Editora Política/La Habana, 1999

Translation: *ESTI*
Editing: *Iraida Aguirrechu* e *Nora Madan*
Design: *Alejandro Greenidge*
Composition: *ESTI* and *Ramón Caballero*

ISBN 959-01-0332-4 (Spanish)
ISBN 959-01-0339-1

Editora Política
Fax (537)811024
Belascoaín No. 864, Havana, Cuba

TO ALL THOSE KIND AND PATIENT ENOUGH TO READ THIS MATERIAL

This speech, delivered at the main lecture hall of the University of Venezuela, is especially significant for me. I delivered it just a month and a half ago, on February 3, 1999.

I do not know how many mortals have had such a special and unique experience as I lived that afternoon.

After a spectacular political victory and supported by a gulf of people, a new young President had been inaugurated only 24 hours before. During the visit I paid to that country on the occasion, together with many other guests, the authorities and students of the aforementioned university insisted that I deliver what people call a Master Lecture. The sole qualifier is embarrassing and gives rise to angst, especially to those of us who are not academics nor have mastered anything beyond the humble craft of using words to say what we think in our own personal way and style.

After overcoming my perennial resistance to such adventures, I agreed to the engagement, always risky and delicate for someone who, as an official guest, visits a country in full political excitement. Furthermore, I was inexorably compelled by the unchanged solidarity towards Cuba of those inviting me to speak. I had been there once already and never forgot it. I felt as if I was going to meet the same people again.

Only as I was about to leave for the campus something struck my mind: time goes by and we do not realize it.

Exactly forty years and ten days had gone by since I had had the privilege of speaking to the students in the imposing main lecture hall of the same militant and prestigious University of Venezuela, on January 24, 1959. One day before, on January 23, 1959 that year, I had arrived in Venezuela. It was the first anniversary of the peoples triumph over an authoritarian military government. Only three weeks before we had achieved our own revolutionary triumph on January 1st, 1959. A huge crowd awaited me at the airport and followed me everywhere during my stay. There was no difference with the experience lived in my own homeland.

I am trying to recall precisely what was going on inside of me. Such a rich mixture of ideas, feelings, and emotions coming from my mind and from my heart! In that confusion of recollections I rather rely on logic than on my memory.

I was 32 years old. In 24 months and 13 days we had overcome a force of 80 thousand men; we had started with 7 rifles, gathered after the great setback of our small group of 82 men, three days after our landing, on December 2, 1956.

1

Full of ideas and dreams but still very inexperienced, we took part in a gigantic rally held on January 23 at Plaza del Silencio. The next day we visited the National University, a traditional bulwark of the Venezuelan people's intelligence, rebelliousness and struggles. Personally, I still felt like the young graduate who had left the university only 8 years before. Since the treacherous March 10, 1952 coup détat, we had spent almost 7 of those 8 years preparing for armed rebellion, in prison, in exile, in our return and successful warfare, without ever losing touch with our university students.

That time I spoke to University professors and students of liberating the oppressed peoples of Our America. Now I was coming back with the same revolutionary fever and 40 years of experience in the epic struggle of our people against the mightiest and most selfish power ever.

Nevertheless, I was facing a great challenge. These were other University professors and students, another Venezuela and another world. What did these young people think? What would their concerns be? To what extent did they agree or disagree with the current process? To what extent were they aware of the objective situation in the world and their own country? I had accepted the kind and friendly invitation upon arrival in Venezuela two days before. I did not even have the minimum amount of time to inform myself properly. What were their interests? What was I going to tell them? How much freedom to speak could a state guest have when attending the inauguration of a new government? I felt compelled by a fundamental respect for the sovereignty and pride of the country that began our wars of independence to avoid interference in its domestic affairs. How would the most diverse social media, institutions and political parties interpret my words? Still, I had no other choice but to talk and I had to do it with complete honesty.

With some facts in mind, four or five pages of references that had to be typed for exact quoting and three or four basic ideas, I headed resolutely for my meeting with the students. I had been asked to hold the rally outdoors so that there would be more space. I insisted on the convenience of meeting indoors, in the main lecture hall, as the ideal place —in my opinion— to meditate and communicate.

When I reached the campus I saw thousands of chairs in different open spaces, full of students who, in front of huge screens, wanted to watch the lecture. The 2800 seats of the main lecture hall were occupied. The ordeal began. I spoke with candor and, at the same time, with full respect for the rules I felt I should respect. I expressed my essential ideas. In summary: what I think about neo-liberal globalization and how absolutely unsustainable the economic order imposed on humankind is, both socially and environmentally. Also its origin designed by imperialist interests and encouraged by the progress of productive forces and scientific and technological breakthroughs as well as its temporary nature and inevitable demise for historical reasons. Likewise, the swindling of the world and the unimaginable privileges usurped by the United States. A special emphasis was made on the significance of ideas and the demoralization and uncertainty of neo-liberal theoreticians. The

2

strategies and tactics for struggle, probable course of events and our full confidence in mans ability to survive were also analyzed.

Here and there I told anecdotes, stories, and small autobiographical references that came up spontaneously in the course of my reflections; that was the absolutely non-Master Lecture I gave. With my usual passion and devotion and greater conviction than ever, I shared the ideas I uphold with cold and reflexive fanaticism. As a combatant who during the long 1959-99 period has not stopped fighting for a minute, I had had the rare privilege of meeting in a historical and renowned University with two different generations of students in two radically different worlds. Both times I was received with the same warmth and respect.

After all the emotions I have lived through I should have been accustomed, but I was not.

Hours had gone by. At the end, I promised that when we meet again, in forty years time, I would be briefer. Many from the enthusiastic and militant crowd stayed in their seats until the end following my words with interest and attention; others left. Perhaps, it was too late. I shall never forget that meeting.

March 18, 1999

MASTER LECTURE DELIVERED BY H.E. DR. FIDEL CASTRO RUZ, PRESIDENT OF THE REPUBLIC OF CUBA, AT THE MAIN LECTURE HALL IN THE CENTRAL UNIVERSITY OF VENEZUELA

FEBRUARY 3, 1999.

I do not have a written speech, unfortunately (*laughter*), but I brought some notes that I thought would be useful for the sake of precision. Still, I have realized that a booklet is missing, one that I had read, underlined, noted with great care and then... left at my hotel (*Laughter and applause*). I have sent for it, and I hope they find it because this copy here is not underlined.

At least I should address this audience formally, shouldn't I? (*Laughter.*) I am not going to make a long list of the many excellent friends we have here. (*Someone in* the audience says: "We cannot hear!") Listen, I do not have that much voice (*laughter and applause*) and if I start shouting... I thought there were better microphones here (*laughter*).

How many of you cannot hear over there? Please, raise you hands. (*Hands raised* raised) If someone does not fix this, we can invite you to sit around here or some place where you can hear (*applause*).

I am going to try to get closer to this small microphone, right? But allow me to begin properly.

Dear friends (*applause*).

I was going to say that today, February 3, 1999, it is 40 years and 10 days to this day that I first visited this university and we met in this same place. Of course, you understand that I am moved —without the melodrama you find in certain soap operas at the moment— (*laughter*) as it would have been unimaginable then that one day, so many years later, I would return to this place.

Several weeks ago, on January 1st, 1999, on the occasion of the fortieth anniversary of the triumph of the Revolution, I stood on the same balcony where I had spoken on January 1st, 1959 in Santiago de Cuba. I was reflecting with the audience gathered there that the people of today are not the same people who were there at the time because of the 11 million Cubans we are today, 7 190 000 were born after that date. I said that they were two different people and yet, one and the same eternal people of Cuba.

I also reminded them that the immense majority of those who were 50 years old then are no longer alive, and that those who were children at that time are over 40 today.

So many changes, so many differences, and how special it was for us to think that there was the people that had started a profound revolution when they were practically illiterate, when 30% of adults could not read or write and perhaps an additional 50% had not reached fifth grade. We estimated that with a population of almost 7 million, possibly little over 250 000 people had gone beyond fifth grade while today the university graduates alone amount to 600 000, and there are almost 300 thousand teachers and professors.

I told my fellow countrymen —in paying tribute to the people who had achieved that first great triumph 40 years before— that in spite of an enormous educational backwardness, they had been able to undertake and defend an extraordinary revolutionary feat. Something else: Probably their political culture was lower than their educational level.

Those were times of brutal anti-communism, the final years of McCarthyism, when by all possible means our powerful and imperial neighbor had tried to sow in the minds of our noble people all possible lies and prejudices. Oftentimes, I would meet a common citizen and ask him a number of questions: whether he believed we should undertake a land reform; whether it would be fair for families to own the homes for which at times they paid big landlords almost half their salaries. Also if he believed that it was right that all those banks where the people's money was deposited should be owned by the people in order to finance with those resources the development of the country instead of being owned by private institutions. Whether those big factories —most of them foreign-owned— should belong to, and produce for, the people... things like that. I could ask ten, fifteen similar questions and he would agree absolutely: "Yes, it would be great."

In essence, if all those big stores and all those profitable business that only enriched their privileged owners belonged to the people and were used to enrich the people, would you agree? "Yes, yes", he would answer immediately. He agreed completely with each of these simple proposals. So, then I asked him: "Would you agree with socialism?" (*Applause*). Answer: "Socialism? No, no, no, not with socialism." Let alone communism... There was so much prejudice that this was an even more scaring word.

Revolutionary legislation was what contributed the most to creating a socialist consciousness in our people. Then, it was that very people —illiterate or semi-illiterate at the beginning— who had to start by teaching many of its children to read and write. The same people that out of love for liberty and yearning for justice had overthrown the tyranny and carried out, and heroically defended, the most profound social revolution in this Hemisphere.

In 1961, only two years after the triumph, with the support of young students working as teachers about 1 million people learned how to read and write. They went to the countryside, to the mountains, the remotest places and there they taught people that were even 80 years old how to read and write. Later on, there were follow-up courses and the necessary steps were taken in a constant effort to attain what we have today. A revolution can only be born from culture and ideas.

No people become revolutionary by force. Those who sow ideas have no need to suppress the people ever. Weapons in the hands of that same people are used to fight those abroad who try to take away their achievements.

Forgive me for touching on this issue because I did not come here to preach socialism or communism and I do not want to be misinterpreted. Nor did I come here to propose radical legislation or anything of the sort. I was simply reflecting on our experience that showed us the importance of ideas, the importance of believing in man, the importance of trusting the people. This is extremely important when mankind is facing such complicated and difficult times.

Naturally, on January 1st this year in Santiago de Cuba it was fitting to acknowledge, in a very special way, that that Revolution which had managed to survive 40 years and mark this anniversary without folding its banners, without surrendering, was mainly the work of the people gathered there, young people and mature men and women. They had received their education under the Revolution and were capable of that feat, thus writing pages of noble and well-earned glory for our nation and our brothers and sisters in the Americas.

We could say that thanks to the efforts of three generations of Cubans, vis-a-vis the mightiest power, the biggest empire ever in Man's history, this sort of miracle came true: that a small country would undergo such an ordeal and achieve victory.

Our even greater recognition went to those countrymen who in the past 10 years —the latest 8 years, to be precise— had been willing to withstand the double blockade resulting from the collapse of the socialist camp and the demise of the USSR which left our neighbor as the sole superpower in a unipolar world, unrivalled in the political, economic, military, technological and cultural fields. I do not mean the value of their culture but rather the tremendous power they exercise to impose their culture on the rest of the world (*applause*).

However, it was unable to defeat a united people, a people armed with just ideas, a people endowed with a great political consciousness because that is most important for us. We have resisted everything and are ready to continue resisting for as long as need be (*applause*) thanks to the seeds planted throughout those decades, thanks to the ideas and the consciousness developed during that time.

It has been our best weapon and it shall remain so, even in nuclear times. Now that I mention it, we even had experiences related to that type of weapons because at a given moment, who knows how many bombs and how many nuclear missiles were aimed at our small island during the well-known Missile Crisis in October 1962. Even in times of smart weapons —which sometimes make mistakes and strike 100 or 200 km away from their targets (*laughter*) but which have a certain degree of precision— man's intelligence will always be greater than any of these sophisticated weapons (*applause and exclamations*).

The type of fight becomes a matter of concepts. The defense doctrine of our nation, which feels stronger today as it has perfected these concepts, is based on the conclusion that at the end —the end of our invaders— it would be a body combat, a man-to-man and a woman-to-invader combat, whether man or woman (*prolonged applause*).

We have had to wage, and will have to continue waging, a more difficult battle against that extremely powerful empire: a ceaseless ideological battle that they stepped up with all their resources after the collapse of the socialist camp when fully confident in our ideas we decided to continue forward. More than that, to continue forward alone; and when I say alone I am thinking of state entities, without ever forgetting the immense and invincible support and solidarity of the peoples which we always had and which makes us feel under a greater obligation to struggle (*applause*).

We have accomplished honorable internationalist missions. Over 500 000 Cubans have taken part in such hard and difficult missions. The children of that people which could not read or write developed such a high consciousness that they shed their sweat, and even their blood, for other peoples; in short, for any people in the world (*applause*).

When the special period began we said: "Now, our first internationalist duty is to defend this bulwark." We meant what Martí had described in the last words he wrote the day before his death, when he said that the main objective of his struggle had to go undeclared in order to be accomplished. Martí, who was not only a true believer in his ideas but also a wholehearted follower of Bolívar's (*applause*), had set himself an objective. According to his own words, it was "to timely prevent with the independence of Cuba that the United States should expand itself over the Antilles and fall, with this additional might, on our lands in the Americas. Everything I have done up so far, and everything I will do, is for this purpose". (*Applause.*)

It was his political will and he expressed his life's aspiration: to prevent the fall of that first trench which the northern neighbors had so many times tried to occupy. That trench is still there, and will continue to be there, with a people willing to fight to death to prevent the fall of that trench of the Americas (*applause*). The people there is capable of defending even the last trench, and whoever defends the last trench and prevents anyone from taking it begins, at that very moment, to attain victory (*applause*).

Comrades, if you allow me to call you that. That is what we are at this moment and I also believe that here, at this moment, we are defending a trench (*applause*). And trenches of ideas —forgive me for quoting Martí again— are worth, as he said, more than trenches of stones (*applause*).

We must discuss ideas here, and so I go back to what I was saying. Many things have happened in these 40 years but the most transcendental is that the world has changed. This world of today in which I am talking —to you to those who had not been born then, and many were far from being born at the time— does not resemble the world of those days.

I tried to find a newspaper where there might be a note on that rally at the university. Fortunately, we do have the complete text of the speech delivered at Plaza del Silencio. The revolutionary fever we had come down with from the mountains only a few days before accompanied us when speaking of revolutionary processes in Latin America and focusing on the liberation of the Dominican people from Trujillo's clutches. I believe that issue took most of the time —or a good part of the time of that meeting— with a tremendous enthusiasm shared by all.

Today, that would not be an issue. Today, there is not one particular people to liberate. Today, there is not one particular people to save. Today, a whole world, all of mankind needs to be liberated and saved (*applause*). And it is not our task, it is *your* task (*applause*).

There was not a unipolar world at that time, a single, hegemonistic superpower. Today, the world and all mankind are under the domination of an enormous superpower. Nonetheless, we are convinced that we will win the battle (*applause*) without panglossian optimism —I believe that is a word writers sometimes use (*laughter*). I believe so because you can be sure that if you drop this notebook (*showing it*) it will fall in a second, that if this table were not here, this notebook would be on the floor. And the table on which this mighty superpower ruling a unipolar world is objectively standing, is disappearing (*applause*).

These are objective reasons, and I am sure mankind will provide all the indispensable subjective ones. For this, neither nuclear weapons nor big wars are necessary but ideas (*applause*). This I say on behalf of that small country we mentioned before, which has struggled staunchly and unhesitatingly for 40 years (*applause*).

You were saying, calling —to my embarrassment— the name by which I am known, I mean "Fidel", because I do not have any other title actually. I understand that protocol demands the use of "His Excellency the President" and so on and so forth. (*Applause and calls of Fidel! Fidel!*) When I heard you chanting: "Fidel! Fidel! What is it with Fidel that Americans cannot put him down?" I had an idea. So I turned to my neighbor on the right, I mean on the right in terms of geography (*laughter and exclamations*), there are some people making signs I do not understand, but I say that all of us are in the same combat unit (*applause*). So, I told him: "Well, actually what they should be asking is: What is it with the Americans that cannot put him down?" (*Laughter and applause.*) And, that instead of saying "him" when asking: "What is it with the Americans that cannot put him down?" They could say: "What is with the Americans that cannot put Cuba down?" It would be more accurate (*applause*). I realize words are used to symbolize ideas. That is the way I have always understood it. I never take credit, nor can I take credit, for that myself. (*Exclamations of "long live Fidel!"*)

Yes, we all hope to live long, all of us! (*Applause*) In the ideas that we believe and in the conviction that those following in our steps will carry them forward. However, your task —it should be said— will be more difficult than ours.

I was saying that we are living in a very different world. This is the first thing we need to understand; then, I was explaining certain political characteristics. Furthermore, the world is globalized, really globalized, a world dominated by the ideology, the standards and the principles of neo-liberal globalization.

In our view, globalization is nobody's whim; it is not even anybody's invention. Globalization is a law of history. It is a consequence of the development of the productive forces —excuse me, please, for using this phrase which might still scare some due to its authorship— it is a consequence of scientific and technologic development, so much so that even the author of this phrase, Karl Marx (*applause*), who had great confidence in human talent, possibly was unable to imagine it.

Certain other things remind me of some of the basic ideas of that thinker among great thinkers. It comes to one's mind that even what he conceived as an ideal for human society could never come true —and this is increasingly clear— if it was not in a globalized world. Not for a second did he think that in the tiny island of Cuba —just to give you an example— a socialist society, or the building of socialism would be attempted, least of all so near to such a powerful capitalist neighbor.

But, yes, we have tried. Furthermore, we made it and we have defended it. And we have also known 40 years of blockade, threats, aggression, and sufferings.

Today, since we are the only ones, all the propaganda, all the mass media mastering the world are used by the United States in the ideological and political warfare against our revolutionary process in the same way as it uses its immense power in all fields —mainly the economic— and its international political influence in the economic warfare against Cuba.

We say "blockade", but blockade does not mean much. I wish it were an economic blockade! What our country has been enduring for a long time is true economic warfare. Do you want evidence? You can go anywhere in the world, any factory owned by an American company, to buy a cap or a kerchief to export to Cuba. Even if produced by nationals of the country in question with raw materials originated in the same country, the United States government thousands of miles away, bans the sale of such a cap or kerchief. Is that blockade or economic warfare?

Do you want an additional example? If by any chance one of you wins the lottery —I do not know if you have lottery here— or finds a treasure, that is possible, and decides to build a small factory in Cuba, you can be sure of receiving very soon the visit of a senior American diplomat, perhaps even the ambassador himself. He will try to persuade you, put pressure or threaten with reprisals so that you do not invest your little treasure in a small factory in Cuba. Is it blockade or economic warfare?

Neither does it allow the sale of medicine to Cuba, even if that medicine is indispensable to save a life, and we have had many examples of such cases.

We have withstood that warfare and like in all battles —whether military, political or ideological— there are casualties. There are those who may be confused, some really are, softened or weakened by a combination of economic difficulties, material hardships, the parading of luxury in consumer societies and the nicely sweetened but rotten ideas about the fabulous advantages of their economic system, based on the mean notion that man is an animal moved only by a carrot or when beaten with a whip. We might say that their whole ideological strategy is based on this.

There are casualties, but also, like in all battles and struggles, other people gain experience, fighters become veterans, multiply their qualities and help preserve and increase the morale and strength needed to continue fighting.

We are winning the battle of ideas (*applause*). Still, the battlefield is not limited to our small island, although the small island has to fight. Today, the world is the battlefield; it is everywhere, in all continents, in all institutions, in every forum. This is the good side of the globalized struggle (*laughter and applause*). We must defend the small island while fighting throughout the huge world they dominate or try to dominate. In many fields they dominate it almost exclusively but not in all fields, nor in the same way, nor in absolutely every country.

They have discovered very intelligent weapons but we, the revolutionaries, have discovered an even more powerful weapon, more powerful: man thinks and feels (*applause*). We have learned that around the world, in the countless internationalist missions we have discharged in one field or another throughout the world. Suffice it to mention a single figure: 26 000 Cuban doctors have taken part in them.

The country that was left with only 3000 out of the 6000 doctors it had at the triumph of the Revolution, many of them unemployed but always wanting to migrate to obtain such and such income and salaries. The Revolution has been able to multiply those 3000 who stayed by training more and more doctors from those who began studying first or second grade in the schools immediately established throughout the country after the Revolution. These people have such a spirit of sacrifice and solidarity that 26 000 of them have accomplished internationalist missions (*applause*) just as other hundreds of thousands Cubans have worked as professionals, teachers, constructors and combatants. Yes, combatants, and we take pride in saying this (*applause*) because fighting against the fascist and racist soldiers of apartheid and contributing to the victory of African peoples to whom that system was the greatest insult is, and will forever be, a reason to feel proud (*applause*).

But in this ignored —highly ignored— effort we have learned a lot from peoples. We have come to know those peoples and their extraordinary qualities. Among other things we have learned, not only through abstract notions but also in ordinary everyday life, that all men may not be equal in their features but all men are equal in their talents, feelings and other virtues. This proves that, in terms of moral, social, intellectual and human abilities, all men are genetically equal (*applause*).

Many have made the big mistake of taking themselves for a superior race.

I was saying that life has taught us many things, and this is what nurtures our faith in the people, our faith in man. We did not read this in a little book, we have lived through it; we have had the privilege of living through it (*applause*).

I have elaborated a bit on these first ideas because of the lost booklet and the microphone problems (*laughter*) so I will have to be briefer on other topics. Yes, I should to be briefer, among other things, for personal reasons. Later, I will have to revisit what I said here (*laughter*), check if a comma or a dot are missing, if any data was wrong. I can assure you that for every hour of speech —which may seem easy— two and three hours of revision are needed, going over it once again. A word might be missing. I never remove an idea I have expressed but at times I have to complete it or add a supplementary concept because oral language differs from written language. If I point out to my neighbor, whoever reads it in a paper does not understand anything (*laughter*), or almost anything. Written language only has exclamation and quotation marks (*laughter*) while the tone, the hands, the soul you put into things cannot be put in writing.

I realized this difference and now we take good care in transcribing and reviewing papers because the issues we discuss can be important, objectively speaking. Besides, one needs to be extremely careful with a great number of things you cannot even think of.

At a given moment, while I was thinking of the rally I was going to have with you at 5 p.m., I asked myself: What am I going to tell the students? (*Applause*). I cannot mention any names, with few exceptions. I can hardly mention any country because at times when I say something in the best of intentions to illustrate an idea I run the risk of being immediately misquoted and then broadcast throughout the world creating a lot of diplomatic problems (*applause*). And since we have to work together in this global struggle, we cannot make it easy for the enemy and its well-designed and efficient propaganda mechanisms to carry out their permanent work of planting confusion and misinformation. They have done a lot already but not enough, you see? (*Laughter*). I have to limit myself a lot for these reasons and I apologize for it.

There is no need here for an extensive explanation on what neo-liberalism is all about. How can I summarize it? Well, I would say this, for instance: Neo-liberal globalization wants to turn all countries, especially all our countries, into private property.

What will be left for us of their enormous resources? Because they have accumulated an immense wealth not only looting and exploiting the world but also working the miracle alchemists longed for in the Middle Ages: turning paper into gold. At the same time, they have turned gold into paper (*laughter*) and with it they buy everything, everything but souls —more accurately said— everything but the overwhelming majority of souls. They buy natural resources, factories, whole communication systems, services, and so on. They are buying even land around the world assuming that being cheaper than in their own countries it is a good investment for the future.

I wonder: What is it they are going to leave us after turning us practically into second class citizens —pariahs would be a more precise term— in our own countries? They want to turn the world into a huge free-trade zone, it might be more clearly understood this way because, what is a free-trade zone? It is a place with special characteristics where taxes are not paid; where raw materials, spare parts and components are brought in and assembled or various goods produced, especially in labor-intensive sectors. At times, they pay not more than 5% of the salary they must pay in their own countries and the only thing they leave us with are these meager salaries.

Sadder still: I have seen how they have put many of our countries to compete with one another by favoring who offer more advantages and tax exemptions to investments. They have put many Third World countries to compete with one another for investments and free-trade zones.

There are countries —I know them— enduring such poverty and unemployment that they have had to establish dozens of free-trade zones as an option within the established world order. It is this or not having even free-trade zone factories and jobs with certain salaries, even if these amount to only 7%, 6%, 5% or less of the salaries the owners of those factories would have to pay in the countries they come from.

We stated this at the World Trade Organization, in Geneva, several months ago. They want to turn us into a huge free-trade zone, yes, that precisely, then with their money and technologies they will start buying everything. It remains to be seen how many airlines will remain national property, how many shipping lines, how many services will remain the property of the people or the nations.

That is the future we are offered by the neo-liberal globalization. But you should not think that is offered to the workers only. It is also being offered to the national businessmen and to the small and medium-size owners. They will have to compete with the transnational companies technologies, with their sophisticated equipment, and their world-wide distribution networks; then, look for markets without the substantial trade credits their powerful competitors can use to sell their products.

We in Cuba can have a great factory, let's say a fridge factory. We have one but it is not great and it is far from being the most modern in the world. It suits us well down there, of course, with warm weather raising in the tropics. Let us assume that other Third World countries manufacture fridge of acceptable quality and even at a lower cost. Their powerful competitors constantly renew their designs, invest huge sums of money to lend prestige to their trade marks, manufacture in many free-trade zones paying low wages or anywhere else, tax-free. They also have abundant capital or financial mechanisms for credits that can be repaid in 1, 2 or 3 years, whatever. They dump the market with electric appliances produced in a world riddled with anarchy and chaos in the distribution of investment capital, under the generalized motto of export-based growth and development, as the IMF advises.

What space is there left for national industries? How can they export and to whom? Where are the potential consumers among the billions of poor, hungry and unemployed living in a large part of the globe? Shall we have to wait until all of them can buy a fridge, a TV set, a telephone, an air conditioner, a car, a PC, a house, a garage, fuel and electricity or until they get an unemployment subsidy, market shares and a safe pension? Is that the path leading to development, as they tell us millions of times by all possible means? What will happen to the domestic market if the accelerated reduction of customs barriers —an important source of budget revenues in many Third World countries— is imposed on them?

Neo-liberal theoreticians have been unable to solve, for instance, the serious problem of unemployment in most of the rich countries, let alone the developing countries, and they shall never find a solution under such a ridiculous conception. It is a huge contradiction in the system that the more they invest and resort to technology, the more people are left jobless. Labor productivity and the most sophisticated equipment born out of human talent multiply material wealth as well as poverty and layoffs, what good are they to mankind? Perhaps to help reduce working hours, have more time for resting, leisure, sports, cultural and scientific upgrading? That is impossible because the sacred market laws and competition patterns —increasingly more imaginary than real— in a world of transnationals and megamerges do not allow it at all. Anyway, who are competing and against whom? Monopoly-and-merger-oriented giants against giants. There is not a place or a corner in the world for the other alleged players in this competition. For wealthy countries, state-of-the-art industries; for Third World workers, manufacturing jeans, tee-shirts, garments, shoes; planting flowers, exotic fruits and other products increasingly demanded in industrialized societies because they cannot be grown there. We know that in the United States, for instance, they even grow marijuana in greenhouses (*laughter and applause*) or in courtyards, and that the value of the marijuana produced in that country is higher than all their corn production, although they are the biggest corn producers in the world (*laughter*). In the long run, their laboratories are, or will wind up being, the biggest narcotics producers in the globe, for the time being under the label of sedatives, anti-depressants and other types of tablets and products which young people have learned to combine and mix in various ways.

In the happy developed world, tough agricultural tasks like picking tomatoes —for which a perfect machine has not yet been invented, a robot capable of picking them according to ripeness, size and other characteristics— cleaning the streets and other unpleasant jobs that nobody wants to do in consumer societies, how do they solve this? Oh! That is what Third World immigrants are for! They themselves do not do that type of work.

For those of us turned foreigners inside our own borders —as I already said— what they leave is the manufacturing of blue jeans and things like that. Under their "wonderful" economic laws, they make us produce blue jeans as if the world population already was 40 billion and every person had enough money to buy a pair of jeans. I am not criticizing the garment; it is very becoming to young people, more so in the case of young women (*laughter and applause*). No, no, I am not criticizing the garment I am criticizing the jobs they want to leave for us and that has absolutely nothing to do with high technology. So, our universities will become redundant and be left to train low cost technical staff for the developed world.

You may have read in the press these days that the United States, in view of the needs of their computer, electronic, etc., etc. industries has decided to acquire in the international market —actually the Third World— and grant visas to 200 000 highly-skilled workers for their state-of-the-art industries. You had better be careful because they are looking for trained people (*laughter*). This time it is not to pick tomatoes. They are not very literate, and many people can see this when they confuse Brazil with Bolivia or Bolivia with Brazil (*laughter and applause*), or when surveys show that they do not even know many things about the very United States. They do not even know if a Latin American country they have heard of is in Africa or Europe, and this is not an overstatement (*laughter and applause*). They do not have all the geniuses or highly skilled workers for their state-of-the-art industries, so they come to our world and recruit a few who are then lost for our countries, forever.

Where are the best scientists of our countries, in which laboratories? Which of our countries has laboratories for all the scientists it could train? How much can we pay that scientist and how much can they pay?

Where are they? I know many outstanding Latin Americans who are there. Who trained them? Oh! Venezuela, Guatemala, Brazil, Argentina, any Latin American country did but they have no possibilities in their homeland. Industrialized countries have the monopoly of laboratories and the money. They recruit them and take them away from poor nations. But not only scientists, athletes too. They would like to buy our baseball players the way slaves were sold on one of those stands, I do not remember what they are called... (*Laughter and applause.*)

They are treacherous. Since there is always a soul to be tempted. So says the Bible, and that referring to the first human beings that were supposed to be better, right? Because supposedly they were not so wicked nor were they familiar with consumer societies. In those days there was no dollar. All of a sudden, even an athlete who is not absolutely first rate, gets paid a couple of millions, or four, five or six millions, he is given an enormous publicity and since Big League batters seem to be so bad, they have some success. I mean no offense for American professional athletes; they are hard working, highly motivated people. Also a commodity bought and sold in the market, although at a high price, but there must be shortcomings in their training because they smuggle in some Cuban pitchers —who, would rank first, second or third— or a shortstop, or a third base. These get there and the pitcher strikes out their best batters and the shortstop does not let a ball go past him (*applause and exclamations*).

We would be practically rich if we auctioned Cuban baseball players (*laughter and applause*). They no longer want to pay American baseball players because those are too expensive. They have organized academies in our countries to train players at a very low cost and pay them lower salaries, but still a salary of millions of dollars a year. Together with this, all the TV advertising, plus automobiles from here to there (*points out*) and beautiful women from all ethnic groups linked to automobile advertising (*laughter*) and the rest of the commercial advertising you see in some tabloids can tempt more than one of our countrymen.

In Cuba we do not spend any newsprint or other resources in such frivolous advertising. The very few times I watch American TV, I can hardly stand it because every three minutes it stops for a commercial, sometimes a man working out on an exercise bike which is the most boring thing in the world... (*Applause and exclamations.*) I am not saying it is wrong, I say it is boring. Any program, even soap operas are interrupted in their sweetest moments of love... (*Laughter.*)

In Cuba we buy some soap operas from abroad because we have not been able to cover our needs and some made in Latin American countries are so attractive to the Cuban audience that they even cause people to stop working. At times, we also get good films from Latin America but practically everything circulating in the world is sheer Yankee-made, canned culture.

Actually, what little paper we have in our country is used for textbooks and for our few newspapers with few pages. We cannot use resources to print those glossy magazines —I do not know what they are called— with many pictures, read by beggars in any street of our capitals, advertising those fancy cars with their beautiful escorts and even a yacht and other things, right? (*Laughter.*) That is how they poison people with propaganda, so that beggars are also cruelly influenced and made to dream of a Heaven —unattainable for them— offered by capitalism.

As I said, in our country we operate differently. Still, they have an influence with the image of a society that is not only alienating, and economically unequal and unfair but also socially and environmentally unsustainable.

I usually say as an example that if the consumer pattern means that in Bangladesh, India, Indonesia, Pakistan o China there may be an automobile in every household... I apologize to those present who have one. Apparently there is no other choice, there are many avenues and the distances are long here. I mean no criticism but a warning against a model not applicable in a world that has yet to develop (*laughter*). You will surely understand me because Caracas cannot accommodate many more cars. You know they are going to have to build avenues three or four stories high (*laughter*). I can imagine that if they were to do the same in China, then the 100 million hectares of arable land would have to be transformed into highways, gas stations and parking-lots leaving practically no space to grow a single grain of rice.

The consumption pattern they are imposing on the world is sheer madness, chaotic and absurd (*applause*).

It is not that I think the world should become a monastery (*laughter*). However, I do believe that the planet has no other choice but to define which are going to be the consumption standards or patterns, both attainable and obtainable, in which mankind should be educated.

Everyday, a lower number of people are reading books. And why should human beings be deprived, for example, of the pleasure of reading a book, or of many other satisfactions in the field of culture and recreation, not only for the sake of acquiring material wealth but also spiritual richness? I am not thinking about men and women working, as in the times of [Frederick] Engels, for 14 or 15 hours a day. I am thinking of men and women working 4 hours a day. If technology so allows it, then why work 8 hours? It is only logical that, as productivity increases, less physical and mental effort will be required; that there be less unemployment and the people have more spare time (*Applause.*)

Let us call a free man he who does not need to work all week, Saturdays, Sundays or double shifts included, to make ends meet, dashing at all hours in large cities, rushing to the subway or to take a bus... Whom are they going to convince that that is a free man? (*Applause.*)

If computers and automatic machines can work wonders in terms of the generation of material goods and services, then why cannot man benefit from the science that he created with his intelligence for the well-being of humanity?

Why must the person endure hunger, unemployment, early death from curable diseases, ignorance, the lack of culture and all sorts of human and social afflictions for exclusively commercial reasons and profits? Why, for the sole interest of an over-privileged and powerful elite operating under frenzied economic laws and institutions which are not, were not, and will not be eternal?

Such is the case of the well-known market laws. The market has become today an object of idolatry, a sacred word pronounced at all hours. Why should this be so when it is possible to generate all the wealth required for meeting reasonable human needs compatible with the preservation of nature and life on our planet? We must ponder and reach our own conclusions. Obviously, it is reasonable for people to have food, health, a roof, clothing and education. Also adequate, rational, sustainable and secure transportation means; culture, recreation, a broad variety of options and many more things that could be at the reach of human beings and not, of course, a private jet or a yacht for each of the 9. 5 billion who will live on the planet within 50 years.

They have impaired the human mind.

Thank goodness that these things did not happen back in the days of the Garden of Eden or of Noahs Arc in the Old Testament. I can imagine that life was a bit more peaceful then (*laughter*). Even if they did have a flood, we are also the victims of floods, all too frequently. Observe what happened recently in Central America. No one knows for sure if as a result of all the climatic constraints we might end up buying tickets or standing in line to board an arc (*laughter*).

This is the situation, they have instilled all this in people's minds. They have alienated millions and hundreds of millions of people and made them suffer even more, as those people are unable to meet their basic needs because they do not even have a doctor to see or a school to attend.

I mentioned the anarchic, irrational and chaotic formula imposed by neo-liberalism: the investment of hundreds of billions without rhyme or reason; having tens of millions of workers manufacturing the same things: television sets, computer parts, and clips or chips, whatever they are called... (*laughter*) an endless number of gadgets, including a large numbers of cars. Everyone is doing the same thing.

They have doubled the capacity for manufacturing cars. Who will buy these cars? Buyers can be found in Africa, Latin America and in many other parts of the world. Only that they do not have a dime to buy cars nor gas, or to pay for the highways or repair shops, which would ultimately ruin Third World countries even more by squandering the resources needed for social development while further destroying the environment.

By creating unsustainable consumer patterns in industrialized countries and sowing impossible dreams throughout the rest of the world, the developed capitalist system has caused great injury to mankind. It has poisoned the atmosphere and depleted its enormous non-renewable natural resources, which mankind will need in the future. Please, do not believe that I am thinking of an idealistic, impossible, absurd world; I am merely trying to imagine what a real world and a happier person could be like. It would not be necessary to mention a commodity, it suffices to mention a concept: inequality has made more than 80% of the people on the planet unhappy, and this is no more than a concept. Concepts and ideas are required that will make possible a viable world, a sustainable world and a better world.

I find amusing the writings of many theoreticians of neo-liberalism and neo-liberal globalization. Actually, I have little time to go to the cinema, practically never, or to watch videos, however good they may be. I rather amuse myself reading the articles these gentlemen write (*laughter*). I can see their analysts, their wisest and most perceptive commentators, immersed in many a great contradiction, in confusion and even despair; they want to square the circle. It must be awful for them (*applause*).

I recall that once they showed me a squared figure with two lines on the top like this, one in the middle and another one downwards (*he points*). The object of the game was to draw over the lines with a pencil without lifting it once. I do not know how much time I lost attempting to do it instead of doing my homework or studying math, languages or other subjects. In my childhood days there were no toys like those invented by the industry to entertain children during school time so that they fail their grades but we used to invent games ourselves in which we lost a lot of time.

But they amuse me and I truly enjoy them, at least, I am grateful to them for that (*laughter and applause*) but I am also thankful for what they teach me. And do you know whose articles and analyses humor me the most? Oh, the most conservatives, the ones who do not even want to hear about the State, who want no mention of it, whatsoever. Those who want a Central Bank on the Moon (*laughter*) so that no human being will dare to lower or rise interest rates. It's unbelievable!

They are the ones who make me happiest because when they say certain things, I ask myself: "Am I wrong? Could this article not have been written by a left wing extremist, a radical?" (*Laughter.*) But, what is this? After seeing [George] Soros write book after book and the last one... yes, I had to read that one too. I had no alternative because I reasoned: "Well, this man is a theoretician but he is also an academician and, furthermore, he has I do not know exactly how many billion dollars as a result of speculative operations." This man must know all about this, all the mechanisms and the tricks. However, he entitled his book: *Capitalism Global Crisis*, which is quite something. There he states it with absolute seriousness (*laughter*) and apparently with such a conviction that I said to myself: "Goodness, it seems that I am not the only madman in this world!" (*Laughter.*) Actually, many have expressed similar concerns. I pay more attention to them than to the adversaries of the current World Economic Order.

The leftists want to prove that the system will inevitably collapse (*laughter*). This is only logical since it is their duty and, after all, they are right (*laughter*). However, the others do not want this to happen. They become despondent and write many things when faced with a crisis and all sorts of threats. They baffled. The least you can say is that they have lost faith in their own doctrines.

Then, those of us who decided to resist in solitude... I do not mean geographical solitude but almost complete solitude in the field of ideas because in the aftermath of these disasters there is a skepticism, which is then multiplied by the expert and powerful propaganda machinery of the empire and its allies. All of this causes many people to feel pessimistic and confused since they do not have all the necessary elements for analyzing circumstances from a historical perspective, consequently, they lose hope.

Those first days were truly bitter, and even before that, as we watched how many people, here and there, became turncoats —and I am not criticizing anyone but the coats... (*Laughter and applause.*) Then, again, things change so quickly! Those illusions are now way behind —as we say in Cuba, and I do not know if you also have this saying here— they lasted less than a candy bar at a schoolyard (*laughter*).

They took to the former Soviet Union their neo-liberal and market recipes, causing destruction, truly incredible destruction, disintegrating nations. They brought about the economic and political dismantling of federations of republics reducing life expectancy in some cases by 14 and 15 years, multiplying infant mortality by three to four times and generating social and economic problems which not even a resurrected Dante would dare to imagine.

It is truly pathetic. Those of us who try to be as well-informed as possible about everything that happens everywhere, and we have no other choice but to be more or less well informed, more or less profoundly, otherwise, we would be disoriented. We have what we think is a quite clear notion of the disasters that the market god and its laws and principles have caused. They, together with the recipes that the International Monetary Fund and other neo-colonizing and re-colonizing institutions have recommended and practically imposed on every country. Even wealthy countries like the Europeans have found it necessary to unite and establish a currency so that experts like Soros do not to bring down even the pound sterling. That is a currency not so long ago reigned as a medium of exchange and was the sword and the symbol of a dominating empire that was the master of the worlds reserve currency. All these privileges are now in the hands of the United States while the British had to suffer the humiliation of watching the fall of their pound sterling.

Such was the case of the Spanish *peseta*, the French franc and the Italian lira; they staked their bets on the immense power of their billions because these speculators are gamblers who play with marked cards. They have all the information, the most prominent economists, Nobel Prize laureates, such as the case of the famous company which was one of the most prestigious in the United States, called the Long Term Capital Management. You will have to excuse my "excellent" English pronunciation (*laughter*), but I prefer the title in Spanish, and practically everyone knows it by its original name, which has been hispanicized. With a total fund of almost 4.5 billion dollars, the company mobilized 120 billion for speculative operations.

The Company had two Nobel Prize Laureates on its payroll together with the most experienced computer software producers. And there you have it. The illustrious gentlemen made a mistake because so many unusual things are happening that they did not foresee some of them. For instance, the difference between tréasury bonds at 30 and 29 years was larger than reasonably expected, immediately all the computers and Nobel Prize laureates decided that they had to straddle. Apparently, they had problems with the crisis that ensued, which they did not anticipate. They thought that they had discovered the miracle of a ceaselessly growing Capitalism, without crisis... We are fortunate that this did not occur to them two or three thousand years ago! It was fortunate that it took Columbus some years to discover this Hemisphere (*laughter*), proving the Earth was round. Also that other economic, social and scientific advances were equally delayed since it was on them that such a system, inseparable from its crises, took root, otherwise there would not be any human beings left on this planet. Perhaps there would be nothing left.

Those from the Long-Term, as it is commonly known, made a mistake and lost. It was a disaster and it was necessary to go to their rescue, violating all international, ethical, moral and financial norms that the United States had imposed on the world. The President of the Federal Reserve declared in the Senate that if that fund was not bailed out, there would inevitably be an economic catastrophe, both in the United States and in the rest of the world.

Another question: What kind of economy is that prevailing today where a handful of multi-millionaires can cause an economic catastrophe in the United States and in the world? I do not mean the big ones, not Bill Gates and others like him since Bill Gates' fortune is about fifteen times the initial capital with which Long Term mobilized enormous sums from savers, obtaining loans from over 50 banks. But, oh! The international economy would have collapsed had it not been bailed out. And this was stated by one of the most competent and intelligent persons in the United Sates, the Chairman of the Federal Reserve.

That distinguished gentleman knows more than a thing or two. The problem is that he does not say everything he knows because part of the method consists in a total lack of transparency and strong doses of sedatives in case of panic accompanied by sweet and encouraging words: "Everything is all right, the economy is running smoothly." This is the accepted and always applied technique.

However, the President of the Federal Reserve had to admit before the US Senate that a catastrophe would have occurred if the Fed had not done what it did.

These are the bases of neo-liberal globalization. Do not worry, you may subtract one or 20 more from their fragile structure. What they have created is unsustainable! However, they have caused anguish for many people throughout the world. They have ruined nations with the International Monetary Fund's formula and continue to impoverish countries. They cannot avoid the ruin of these countries, yet they do not cease to do foolish things and in the stock markets they have inflated the prices of shares and continue to do so ad infinitum.

In the U.S. stock markets, more than one third of the families' savings and 50% of the pension funds have been invested in shares. One can imagine the impact of a catastrophe similar to that of 1929, when only 5% of the population had their savings invested in the stock market. Today, they would feel terrified and run in haste. That was what they did in August after the crisis in Russia whose share of the worlds gross product is only 2%. That crisis made the Dow Jones, the key index of the New York Stock Market, fall in one day by more than 500 points; 512 to be exact, causing an enormous commotion.

The truth is that the leaders of this dominating system spend most of their time running around the world, from banks to financial institutions (*laughter*). And when they saw what occurred in Russia, a track and field Olympics ensued. They met with the Council on Foreign Relations in New York. Clinton delivered a speech, stating that recession and not inflation was the real danger. In a matter of days, in practically a few hours, they made a 180 degree shift and instead of increasing interest rates what they actually did was to lower them. On October 5 and 6, all the directors of central banks met in Washington. Speeches were delivered, an undetermined number of criticisms were raised to the Monetary Fund and the so-called measures were adopted to reduce the danger. A few days later the US government met with the G-7, which decided to contribute 90 billion dollars to stop the crisis from extending to Brazil and from there to the rest of South America. They were trying to impede the flames from reaching the over-inflated stock markets of the United States. A small pin, the smallest of holes and the balloon would deflate. These are the risks threatening neo-liberal globalization.

That was what they did. Then some of us, myself included, reflected on it and I said: "They have resources, they have the possibility to maneuver and postpone the great crisis for a time." They could postpone it but not ultimately avoid it. I reflected on the matter and said: "Apparently they have succeeded thanks to all the measures adopted or imposed: lowering interest rates; 90 billion dollars to support the Fund which had no funds (*laughter*); the steps taken by Japan to confront the bank crisis; Brazil's announcement of harsh economic measures and the timely statement that the US economy had grown more than expected in the third quarter."

It seemed that things would hold on. However, only a few days ago, we were again surprised by the news from Brazil on the current economic situation. This truly hurts us very much for reasons connected to this very issue, that is, the effort that our peoples must make to join forces and wage the hard struggle that awaits us. Actually, a destructive crisis in Brazil would have an extremely negative impact on Latin America.

At present, despite everything they did, Brazilians are faced with a complicated economic situation, regardless of the fact that the United States and the international financial institutions used up a large part of their recipes and ammunition. Now, after the first months since the great scare, they are demanding new conditions and seem more indifferent to the fate of Brazil.

As for Russia, they intend to keep it on the brink of an abyss. This is not a small country. It is the largest country in the world with a 146 million population and thousands of nuclear weapons where a social explosion, an internal conflict or any other event can cause terrible damage.

Yet, these gentlemen who manage the world economy are so insane and reckless that, after ruining a country with their recipes, it does not even occur to them to use some of their own printed paper because that is precisely what the Treasury bonds are, a refuge for terrified speculators. When faced with any risk, speculators would buy United States Treasury bonds. It does not occur to them to use some of the 90 billion designed for the Fund in the prevention of an economic or political catastrophe in Russia. What occurs to them is to impose a bunch of impossible conditions. They demand that budgets, which are already below the indispensable limit, be cut. They also demand free conversion and immediate payment of high debts; a host of requirements that would deplete the remaining reserves of any country. They refuse to think, they have not learned their lesson. They intend to maintain that country in a precarious situation, at the edge of the sword, with humanitarian assistance, imposing conditions and generating truly serious dangers.

However, the Russian issue has not been solved. A country they impoverished, thanks to their advisors and formulas. Nor have they solved the Brazilian issue, a problem they were so very much interested in solving, since it could affect them very closely. Therefore it seemed to me, for example, that this was the last stronghold of the United States stock markets.

It was a close call. Some of the aforementioned measures stabilized the situation a bit. Once again the sale and purchase of shares was unleashed and once again they are off on a race to outer space, preparing the conditions for an even greater crisis, and relatively soon. No one knows what the consequences for the US economy and its society will be.

It is impossible to imagine what would occur in the event of another 1929. They believe they have done away with the risk of a crisis like that of 1929, and actually they have solved nothing. They have not even been able to prevent the Brazilian crisis consequently, they may affect the whole integration process in South America, the whole integration process in Latin America and the interests of all our countries.

That was why I said that recently we had received bad news.

However, there is a cause for everything and an explanation, and after waiting and watching how they think, what they say, what they do one can actually guess what is hidden in their minds. The important thing with those people is not so much to believe what they are saying but, based on what they are saying, to penetrate their brains with the least possible trauma as we would not want to harm them (*laughter*) to know what they are actually thinking, to know what they have not said and why they have not said it.

This is how they behave. This is also why it is to us a matter of profound interest, a source of reflection, encouragement and reassertion of our convictions. Because we lived through the days of uncertainty and bitterness that I previously described, and witnessed the loss of faith of many progressive men and women. Now, we can see that the truths are gaining ground and that many people are now beginning to think more profoundly. And those who claimed the end of history and the final victory of their anachronistic and selfish concepts are now in decline and in undeniable demoralization.

These past 8 years —since 1991, in other words, from the collapse of the USSR to date— have been hard years for us in every sense, in this sense as well, in terms of ideas and conceptions. Now we see that the high and mighty, those who thought they had created a system or an empire that would last one thousand years are beginning to realize that the bases of that system, of that empire, are falling apart.

What is the legacy of this global capitalism or of this neo-liberal capitalist globalization? Not only that capitalism that we know from its very sources, that capitalism from which this one was born which was progressive yesterday but reactionary and unsustainable today. A process many of you, historians, and those who are not like the students of economics must know. A history of 250 to 300 years, whose primary theoretician, John Adams, whom you know well, published his book in 1776, the same year of the Declaration of Independence of the United States. He was a great talent, undoubtedly, a great intelligence. I do not think he was a sinner, a culprit or a bandit. He studied the economic system that emerged in Europe while it was in full bloom. He pondered, examined and outlined the theoretical bases of capitalism. The capitalism of his day, because John Adams could have never imagined this one.

On those days of small workshops and factories, Adams felt that the individual interest was the prime motivation of economic activity and that its private and competitive quest constituted the basic source of public welfare. It was not necessary to appeal to man's humanity but his love of himself.

Personal property and management were all that was compatible with the small industrie's world that John Adams knew. He did not even live to see the enormous factories and the impressive masses of workers at the end of the 18th century. He could much less imagine the gigantic corporations and modern transnational companies with millions of shares and managed by professional executives who have nothing to do with the ownership of these entities and whose main function it is to occasionally report to the shareholders. They decide, however, which dividends are paid, how much and where to invest. These forms of property, management and enjoyment of the wealth produced have nothing to do with the world he lived in.

Nevertheless, the system continued to develop and gained considerable momentum during the English Industrial Revolution. The working class emerged and so did Karl Marx, who in my view, with all due respect to those who may be of a different view, was the greatest economic and political thinker of all times. No one learned more about the laws and principles of the capitalist system than Marx. Presently, more than a few members of the capitalist elite, anguished by the current crisis are reading Marx, seeking a possible diagnosis and remedy for the evils of today. Socialism, as the antithesis of capitalism, surfaced with Marx.

The struggle between those ideas symbolized by both men of thought has persisted for many years and still continues. The original capitalism continued to develop under the principles of its most prominent theoretician until approximately World War I.

From before the war, a certain level of globalization existed. There was a gold standard for the international monetary system. In 1929, there was the great crisis followed by the great recession that lasted over 10 years. Then, another important thinker emerged, John Maynard Keynes. He is one of the four pillars of economic thought that had an enormous political impact on the last three centuries and the indelible seal of each of his predecessors. Keynes was a man of advanced ideas for his time, not like Karl Marx's although quite respectful of Marx and coincided with him in certain concepts. He elaborated the formulas that extricated the United States from the great depression.

Of course, he did not do it alone. A group of scholars agreed with him and were under his influence. At that time, there were practically no economists, nor were they taken very seriously. I do not know if this was for better or for worse, it all depends... (*Laughter.*) However, highly trained groups began to surge. They had plenty of statistical information and conducted extensive studies and during the Roosevelt administration in a country that was both exhausted and anguished by endless years of recession; many of them became prominent cabinet members or other. Keynes's theories helped pull capitalism out of the worst crisis it had ever known.

There was a temporary suspension of the gold standard that was later re-established by Roosevelt in 1934, if I remember correctly. I do know, however, that it was maintained until 1971. It must have lasted 37 consecutive years until Mr. Nixon came along and the great empire embezzled us all (*laughter*).

Perhaps you are rightly wondering why I am talking about this. I have mentioned these characters, although I still have not referred to the fourth one, because it is very important to know the history of the system which currently rules the world; its anatomy, principles, evolution and experiences, in order to understand that this creature, which came into being almost three centuries ago, is reaching its final stage (*applause*). It is convenient to know this, and it is almost time to perform an autopsy on it before it finally dies, lest that many of us would die with it, or if this takes too long, that all of us would die as well (*laughter and applause*).

I mentioned the gold standard because it had a lot to do with the problems that we are now confronting. Towards the end of World War II, an attempt was made to establish an institution that would regulate and step up world trade. The economic situation was in shambles as a consequence of the long, destructive and bloody war. Therefore, the well-known Bretton Woods Agreement was established by a number of countries, including the most influential and the wealthiest.

The United States was already the richest nation accumulating 80% of the world gold. A fixed exchange currency was established based on gold, the gold-dollar standard so to say, because gold was combined with the US bank note, which then became the international reserve currency. This gave the United States a special privilege and an enormous power, which it has continued to use in its own best interest. It gave that country the power to manipulate the world economy, set rules, and prevail in the International Monetary Fund where 85% of the votes are required to make any decision. So with its 17.5%, the U.S. may obstruct any decision of that institution. Thus, it controls and is practically the owner of the Fund. It has the last say and has been able to impose worldwide the economic order that we suffer today.

However, Nixon cheated before that. Initially the U.S. had 30 billion dollars in gold whose price was maintained through a strict control of the market at 35 dollars the so-called troy ounce. Soon, it began to incur in tax-free expenditures, tax-free wars. The United States spent more than 500 billion dollars on the Vietnam adventure. By then, they were running out of gold. They only had 10 billion dollars left and, at that pace, they were going to lose it all. In a speech delivered on August 17, 1971, I think, Nixon openly declared that he suspended the US dollar conversion into gold.

As I already explained, they were able to maintain a fixed price for gold thanks to a strict control of the market, the aforementioned 35 dollars an ounce. If there were an excess gold supply in the market they would buy, after all, it did not cost them anything. They would hand over those bank notes and receive gold in exchange, thus avoiding a drop in prices. If an excessive gold demand threatened to raise its price, they would do the opposite. They would sell gold from their abundant reserves, in order to lower its price. Many countries backed their currency with gold reserves or with US bank notes. At least, there was a relatively stable monetary system for trade.

From the moment that Nixon, defrauding the whole world and everyone who owned one of those bills announced that the value of US dollar bills would no longer be received in physical gold he suspended the most sacred commitment undertaken through an international treaty. This is something he did unilaterally, by presidential decree or through some other legal procedure, it was not even a House decision, and the world had hundreds of billions of dollars in the central banks' reserves.

They kept the gold. Later, prices rose. The value of the remaining gold, worth 10 billion dollars, rose to more than the 30 billion dollars they initially had in physical gold. They also kept all privileges of the system, the value of their Treasury bonds and their bank notes that continued to be the compulsory reserve currency in the countries'central banks. In order to get those dollars the countries had to export all their goods, while the United States only had to pay the printing costs. Consequently, the U.S. economic power became even greater, and in exchange, it began to destabilize the world. How? The other currencies suffered fluctuations. Their values changed from day to day. Money speculation was unleashed; speculative sales and purchases of currencies amounting today to colossal sums, based on the constant fluctuation of their values. A new phenomenon had emerged, which is now beyond control.

Currency speculation which only 14 years ago involved 150 billion dollars a year now amounts to more than 1 trillion a day. I would like to point out, so that we may understand each other in this Babel Tower of figures and numbers which often give rise to confusions as well as translation mistakes and misunderstandings, that I am not referring to the term *billón* in Spanish, as there is much confusion between the meaning of *billion* in English and *billón* in Spanish (*laughter*). The former equals one thousand million and the latter one million million. This is what they call a "trillion" in the United States. A new term has just begun to circulate, the *millardo* which also represents one thousand million. I said, and I repeat, in order to avoid any confusion, that the currency speculative operations reached a figure of more than a million million dollars a day, that is, one trillion.

It has grown by two thousand times in 14 years as a result of the measures adopted by the United States in 1971 which caused the fluctuation of all the currencies, either within certain limits or freely. Consequently, we now have this new capitalism, something which would have never occurred to John Adams, not even in his worst nightmares (*laughter*) when he wrote his book on the wealth of nations.

Other new and equally uncontrollable phenomena have emerged —I already mentioned one— the hedge funds. In fact, there are hundreds or thousands of these. Think of what might be happening, and what the repercussions might be, after the Chairman of the US Federal Reserve declared that one of them might have caused an economic cataclysm in the United States and the rest of the world. He is well informed. He should know in detail what is truly happening.

One can guess, judging by certain articles published in a number of conservative magazines because they know. At times, they need to print something that will support their arguments. However, they try to be extremely discreet. But there are no longer so many foolish people in the world (*laughter*) and it is not hard to discern what they did not want to say. A phrase published in a very famous British magazine criticizing the measures adopted by Greenspan in connection with the well-known hedge fund said more or less that perhaps Greenspan had additional information. I cannot exactly recall the phrase used which was more subtle.

However, it is possible to discern from this magazine, which is careful about what it prints and is a highly specialized journal that it knew more than it was saying. And although it did not agree with the decision of the Chairman of the Reserve, it knew perfectly well what he meant when he ascertained that "It is necessary to save this Fund." Undoubtedly, both the magazine and Greenspan knew why the latter felt that there could be a chain of bankruptcies of the most important banks in strategic centers.

The fourth personality who has definitely marked the latest stage of capitalist economic development thinking is Milton Friedman. He is the father of the strict supply-side economics applied by many countries throughout the world and which the International Monetary Fund advocates so strongly: the last recourse against the inflationary phenomenon that surged with extraordinary strength after Keynes.

At present, we can find anything: a number of countries immersed in a depression, others in inflation, recipes and measures that destabilize governments. The world has already realized that the International Monetary Fund will economically ruin and politically destabilize the countries it assists or tries to assist. Now more than ever we can rightly say that the assistance of the International Monetary Fund is like the Devil's kiss (*applause*).

Allow me to point out some facts which I would like to draw to your attention and which respond to the question I asked myself when I said: "What is the legacy of capitalism and neo-liberal globalization?" After 300 years of capitalism, the world now has 800 million hungry people. Now, at this very moment, there are 1 billion illiterates, 4 billion poor, 250 million children who work regularly and 130 million people that have no access to education. There are 100 million homeless and 11 million children under five years of age dying every year of malnutrition, poverty and preventable or curable diseases.

There is a growing gap between the poor and the rich, within countries and between countries; a callous and almost irreversible destruction of nature; an accelerated squandering and depletion of important non-renewable resources; pollution of the air and underground waters, rivers and oceans; climatic changes with unpredictable but already perceptible consequences. During the past century, more than 1 billion hectares of virgin forests were devastated and a similar area has become either deserts or wastelands.

Thirty years ago hardly anyone discussed these issues; now it is crucial for our specie. I do not wish to give any more figures. I believe that these data serve to qualify a system which claims to be perfect, to grant a rating of 100 points, 90, 80, 50, 25 or perhaps less than 25. All this is very easy to demonstrate and its disastrous results may be conceptualized as self-evident truths.

In face of all this, perhaps many are wondering "What is to be done?" Well, the Europeans have invented their own recipe. They are uniting. They spoke about a single currency that has already been approved and is now in the process of implementation. The good wishes of the United States, according to spokespersons of that country, have not been lacking, good wishes which are as great as they are hypocritical (*laughter*) because everyone knows that what they really want is for the Euro to fail. They say, "What a wonderful thing, the Euro is very good, it is an excellent idea." This is the case of a rich, developed Europe with an annual G.D.P. per capita of 20 000 USD in some countries and of 25 000 to 30 000 USD in others. Compare these countries with others in our world with 500, 600 or 1000 USD.

And what shall we do? This is a question that we must all ask ourselves within this context, at a moment when they are trying to swallow our countries. And you can rest assure that this is what they would like to do. We should not expect another miracle like that when the prophet was delivered from the gut of a whale (*laughter*) because if that whale would swallowed us, we are really going to be fully digested at full speed.

Yes, this is our hemisphere and I am here speaking from no other place than Venezuela, Bolivar's glorious homeland (*applause*), where he dreamed, where he conceived the unity of our nations and worked for its attainment at a time when it took three months to travel from Caracas to Lima on horseback and when there were no cellular phones, nor airplanes, nor highways, nor computers, nor anything of the sort. And yet, he realized and foresaw the danger that those few, recently independent colonies, far up North, could pose. He was prophetic when he said, "The United States seem destined by Providence to plague the Americas with misery in the name of liberty." He launched the idea of our people's unity and struggled for it until his death. If it was a dream then, today it is a vital necessity (*applause*).

How can solutions be worked out? They are difficult, very difficult. As I said, the Europeans have set a target and are immersed in a tight competition with our neighbor of the North; this is obvious, a strong and growing competition. The United States does not want anyone to interfere with its interests in what it considers to be its hemisphere. It wants everything absolutely for itself. On the other hand, China in the Far East, is a huge nation and Japan is a powerful, industrial country.

I believe that globalization is an irreversible process and that the problem is not globalization *per se*, but rather the type of globalization. This is why it seems to me that for this difficult and tough undertaking, for which the peoples do not have much time, the Latin Americans are the ones who should hurry the most and struggle for unity, agreements and regional integration not only within Latin America but also between Latin America and the Caribbean (*applause*). There we have our English speaking sister nations of the Caribbean, the CARICOM members, who after barely a few years of independence have acted with impressive dignity.

I say this based on their behavior towards Cuba. When everybody in Latin America, except for Mexico, severed all ties with our country in response to American pressures, the Caribbean nations, together with Torrijos, were the first to break through. They have struggled to break Cuba's isolation until the present when Cuba maintains relations with the immense majority of the Latin American and Caribbean countries (*applause*). We know them and we appreciate them. They cannot be left to their own fate, they cannot be left in the hands of the WTO and its agreements. They cannot be left at the mercy of the US banana transnational enterprises, which try to take away the small preferences that they so badly need. You cannot mend the world by leveling everything to the ground; that is the way the Yankees do it, by razing everything.

Several of these countries live from their plantations and produce only 1% of the banana marketed, 2% at the most, which is meaningless. The United States government, to protect a US transnational that owns three plantations in Central America, filed an appeal with the WTO and won. Now the Caribbean nations are very worried because similar procedures may be applied to take these preferences away and because measures are being adopted to liquidate the Lome Convention, by virtue of which they enjoy some considerations as former colonies and countries in dire need of resources for development. It is unfair to take these considerations away from them.

It is not fair to treat all nations equally, as there are marked differences in their levels of development that cannot be ignored. It is not right to use the same recipe for all. It is not right to impose a single formula. Formulas for controlling and developing economic relations are of no avail if they will only benefit the wealthy and the powerful. Both the IMF and the WTO want everything *tabula rasa*.

The OECD, the exclusive club of the wealthy, was rather secretly preparing a supranational multilateral investment agreement to establish the laws that would govern foreign investment. Something like a world wide Helms-Burton Law, and all that rather very quietly. They had almost everything ready and then a non-governmental organization got hold of a copy of the draft. The copy was disseminated through Internet creating a scandal in France, which rejected such a draft agreement, apparently they had not paid much attention to what was brewing at the OECD. Later, I think the Australians did the same, consequently the draft was abandoned which had been so secretly worked out.

This is how many important and decisive international treaties are produced. Then, they put the draft on the table so that those who want to sign it may do so and those who do not, well, everyone knows what happens to those who do not want to sign (*laughter*). Not a single word was discussed with the countries that were to apply such unavoidable standards. This is how they treat us. This is how they handle the most vital interests of our peoples.

They will continue. We must be very vigilant and alert with these institutions. We must say that they were laying a big trap for us. So far, we have managed to sidestep it but they will continue with their scheming to make our living conditions even worse. It was not only a matter of competing with everyone and with the whole world making desperate concessions in every field. The Agreement on Multilateral Investments was intended to facilitate their investments in the conditions they deem fit, respecting the environment if they wish, or poisoning the rivers in every country if they feel like it, destroying nature without anyone being able to demand anything from them. But Third World countries are a majority in the WTO and, if we can stop them from deceiving and dividing us, we can fight for our interests. Cuba could not be excluded from the WTO because it belonged to it since its foundation.

But they do not want China in, at least they are putting up great resistance (*laughter*). China is making great efforts to enter the WTO because a 1000 percent tariff can be applied to countries not belonging to this institution and their exports can be completely blocked. The richest countries are setting the rules and requirements that better suit them.

What is it that suits them? What is it they are after? They want to see the day when there will be no tariffs, when their investments will not be charged by the tax authorities in any country. They obtain years of tax exemption as a concession from underdeveloped countries thirsty for investments where they get the lion's share and the right to do as they please with their investments in our countries with no restriction whatsoever. They also impose the free circulation of capital and goods throughout the world. Of course, the exception is that commodity bearing the name of Third World people who are the modern slave, the cheap manpower so abundant in our planet, flooding the free-trade zones in their own land or sweeping streets, harvesting vegetables and doing the hardest and worst paid jobs when legally or illegally admitted into the former metropolis or into consumer societies.

This is the type of global capitalism they want to impose. Our countries full of free-trade zones would have no other income but the meager salary of those fortunate enough to get a job, while a bunch of billionaires accumulate fortunes, which no one knows how big they will get.

The fact that an American citizen, no matter how great his talent and expertise in technology and business matters, owns a 64 billion dollar fortune, which is the annual income of more than 150 million human beings in the poorest countries, is something awesomely unequal and unfair. That this capital has been accumulated over a few years, because the stocks value of the large American enterprises doubles every three or four years through stock exchange transactions inflating the value of assets *ad infinitum*, shows a reality that cannot be considered rational, sustainable or endurable. Someone is paying for all that: the world and the astronomic figures of poor, hungry, ill, illiterate and exploited people populating the Earth.

What year 2000 are we going to celebrate and what kind of a new century will we live in? Besides, this century does not end on December 31st. People are self-deceived, because the last year in this century is actually the year 2000 and not 1999. However, there will be celebrations and I believe that some will be very happy to celebrate, in a special way, on December 31, 1999, and on December 31, 2000, and those who sell nougat, beverages, Christmas presents, Santa Clauses and all that will do great business with two end-of-the-century days instead of one (*laughter*). France will sell more champagne than ever.

Its all right with me. I spent this last Christmas Eve writing a speech. It is better that way because you do not fall in the temptation of broaching additional topics and issues and you strictly follow what you have promised yourself. That was what I was doing at midnight, this last Christmas Eve but I was happy. It was the eve of the fortieth anniversary of a revolution they were not able to overcome (*prolonged applause*). I was really happy, I cannot pretend otherwise.

The world will reach that 21st century with people living under New York bridges, wrapped in papers, while others amass enormous fortunes. There are many tycoons in that country but the number of those living under bridges, at the entrance of buildings or in slums is incomparably higher. In the United States millions live in critical poverty, something in which the fanatic advocates of the economic order imposed upon humanity cannot take pride.

A few days ago I was talking with an American delegation visiting Cuba, actually well informed, friendly and outstanding religious people and scientists, and they told me that they were engaged in building a pediatric hospital in the Bronx. I asked them: "Is not there a pediatric hospital in the Bronx?" And they answered: "No." "And how many children are there in the Bronx?" I asked. And they said: "Four hundred thousand children." So there are 400 000 children in a city such as New York, many of them of Puerto Rican descent, of Hispanic descent in general, and Black, who do not have a pediatric hospital.

But they also said that, "There are 11 million American children who do not have medical insurance." They are mostly Black, mixed, natives or the children of Hispanic immigrants. Do not think discrimination in that society is based only on the color of the skin, no, it is not. Whether they have blond or dark hair, they are at times treated with contempt simply because they are Latin American (*applause*).

There was a time when I visited that country, then I sat in cafeterias or lived in those motels at the side of the road and more than once I felt their contempt; they almost felt furious to have a Hispanic around. It impressed me as a society full of hatred.

The 11 million children without medical insurance belong, most of them, to those minorities living in the United States. They have the highest infant mortality rate. I asked them what was the infant mortality rate in the Bronx and they said they thought it was about 20 or 21 per 1000 live births in the first year of life. There are worse places —in Washington itself it is quite high— and in areas where Hispanic immigrants mostly live it is 30 or 30 odds. It is not the same everywhere.

Their infant mortality is higher than that of Cuba. The blockaded country, the country targeted for their war and from which they stole 3000 physicians, today has an infant mortality of 7.1 per every 1000 live births (*applause*). Our rates are better and they are very similar throughout the country. It is 6 in some provinces, not precisely in the capital; it may be 8 in others, but it is within that rank, two or three percentage points of difference with the national average because medical care reaches all social sectors and regions.

Even after the beginning of the special period, in these eight terrible years, we were able to reduce infant mortality to 7.1 from 10 in 1998 (*applause*). It was an almost 30 percent reduction and that even when we entered a very difficult stage after the demise of the socialist camp and especially the Soviet Union, with which we had most of our trade. Also the US economic war against Cuba grew more severe. In 1993, for example, despite all our efforts, the per capita daily calories intake had declined to 1863 from 3000 and to approximately 46 g of animal or plant protein from 75 g. Oh, but among other essentials, a very inexpensive, subsidized litter of milk was guaranteed to children under 7 years of age (*applause*).

We have managed to help the most vulnerable groups. If there is a severe drought or any other natural disaster we try to find resources wherever we can to protect everyone but specially the children and the elderly.

The establishment of new very important scientific centers has been one of the advances of the Revolution during the special period. Our country produces 90 per cent of its medications, even though some raw materials must be imported from very distant places. We have shortages of medications, that is true, but everything possible has been done to always have the most essential ones in stock, to have a central reserve, in case some may be missing one day, and we are trying to have more reserves. These actions had to be taken because we must anticipate in order to be in capacity to protect those in greatest need. Of course, it is also possible to receive medications sent by relatives abroad; we facilitate it as much as possible, we do not charge anything at all, no tariff is paid for that, but we do all we can for the state to offer these resources to all our population.

Despite the said decline in food consumption, we have been able to reduce infant mortality by 30 percent, as I said before. We have also maintained and even raised life expectancy. On the other hand, not a single school was closed (*applause*); not a single teacher lost his job, on the contrary, teacher-training colleges and institutions are open for all those who wish to enroll (*applause*).

I must clarify that we have not been able to do the same in all professions. In Medicine, we have already had to set certain limits, looking for higher qualifications, for a higher quality in those entering the profession because we graduated many physicians in our struggle against our neighbor and we let them migrate if they wanted to. In that battle we established 21 medical colleges (*applause*).

Right now we are offering 1000 scholarships to Central American students to be trained as physicians in our country (*applause*) and an additional 500 each year for ten years; we are establishing a Latin American medical college (*applause and comments*). With the cuts we have made in expenses, even in defense expenses despite the dangers we face, we will be able to locate the medical college in the former facilities of an excellent school for civil and military navy captains and technicians whose school has been moved to another facility. The medical college will be ready in March and the first Central American students will arrive for a six months premedical catch-course to refresh their knowledge and prevent later dropouts. In September more than a thousand Central American students will be studying their first year of Medicine in Cuba (*applause*). I do not know if it is necessary to add that their studies will be absolutely free of charge (*applause*).

Perhaps I should say —and do not take it as an advertisement for Cuba but as something having to do with the ideas about what can be done with very little— that we offered 2000 physicians to the Central American countries hit by hurricane Mitch (*applause*) and we have said that, if a developed country or some developed countries —and some have already answered— supply the medications, our medical personnel is ready to save in Central America every year —I repeat, every year!— as many lives as were lost in the hurricane, supposing the hurricane caused no less that 30 000 casualties, as reported. Twenty-five thousand of those lives to be saved would be children's.

According to estimates medications to save a child often cost only a few cents. What cannot be bought at any price is a trained physician ready to work in the mountains (*applause*), in the remotest places, in swampy areas, full of insects, snakes, mosquitoes and some diseases that do not exist in our country. And none of them hesitate. The immense majority of our physicians have volunteered for that task. They are ready for it and 400 of them are now working in Central America; 250 physicians are already working in Haiti, a country that receive the same offer after it was hit by hurricane Georges.

The percentage of lives that can be saved in Haiti is higher because infant mortality there is 130 or 132. It means that by reducing it to 35 —and in our country we know very well how to do it— 100 children a year for every 1000 live births would be saved. That is why the potential is larger. Its population is 7.5 million, and the birth rate is very high, thus, physicians there may save more lives. In Central America the average rate in the countries hit by the hurricane is about 50 or 60, almost half of the lives that can be potentially saved.

I warn you that these are conservative estimates. There is a margin over and above the figures mentioned. On the other hand, we do not want our physicians working in the cities because we do not want any local physician to be affected in any way by the presence of the Cuban physicians. Cuban physicians offer their services in the places where there are no physicians and where other physicians would not go. On the contrary, we want to have the best relations with local physicians, we want to cooperate with them, whether they are in private practice or not. If they are interested in a case, it is all right with us.

We have said that cooperation with local physicians is necessary and also cooperation with other sectors. Our physicians are not going there to preach political ideas; they are going to accomplish a humane mission. That is their task. There should also be cooperation with priests and pastors, since many of these have been carrying out their work in isolated places. Some of our first physicians to arrive lived in parish facilities.

So they are working in coordination and we are very pleased of it. They are working in intricate places, where there are indigenous people who speak their own language, people with great dignity, and peasants who live in small villages. That facilitates the physician's work because in Cuba peasants live far from each other in the mountains so they must walk long distances to visit the patients regularly while in a village they can visit more than once a day.

A program is being implemented there that says much about what can be done with a minimum of material resources. What is most important and those gentlemen, the managers of the financial institutions I have mentioned do not know it, is that there is a capital worth much more than all their millions: the human capital (*applause*).

Perhaps, one day I meet one of those assistants to Bill Gates, who is a computing champion, then I will ask him a question: Can you tell me how many Americans have served abroad since the Peace Corps was created? Just to know if they are more than the number of Cubans who have done likewise thanks to the generous and cooperative spirit of that very slandered and ignored island and people, against which a war that was not waged against apartheid fascists is being waged. I am speaking about an economic war. I know many decent, altruistic Americans. I know many, and it is a very high merit that so many altruistic people live in a place whose system only sows selfishness and the venom of individualism. I respect these Americans. I have met some that have served with the Peace Corps but I am sure that they have not been able to mobilize, since their creation, the number Cuba has mobilized.

Once, when Nicaragua requested 1000 teachers —later they asked for some more— we invited volunteers and 30 000 offered. Then, when the bandits organized and supplied by the United States who waged that dirty war against the Sandinistas murdered some of our teachers —who were not in the cities, but in the most isolated places in the countryside, sharing the peasants living conditions— 100 000 volunteered to go (applause). This is what I mean! And I must add that most of them were women because women are the majority in that profession (*applause*).

That is why I am discussing idea; that is why I am discussing consciousness. That is why I believe what I am saying, that is why I believe in mankind. Because when so many of our fellow countrymen and women went or were ready to go to those places, consciousness and the idea of solidarity and internationalism proved to be a mass phenomenon (*applause*).

I will complete my idea. I already said that they took half our physicians and more than half of the professors of the only medical college in Cuba. We accepted the challenge —there is nothing like a challenge— and today Cuba has 64 000 physicians, one for every 176 people (*applause*), twice the number of physicians per capita in the most industrialized of all the countries in the First World. And what I did not say is that since the beginning of the special period we have incorporated 25 000 new physicians in health institutions and communities throughout the country in towns, country, plains and mountains. This is really human capital!

It is much easier to conquer a person than to buy it (*applause*). Fortunately, it is much easier, because with its so-called easing of the blockade —actually intended to deceive the world— what the U.S. administration is practically saying is that every American should buy a Cuban (*laughter*). I say: Well, let us raise the price then (*laughter*) because there are 27 Americans for every Cuban. After all it has done against our country, after intensifying its economic war under the pressure of the extreme right, this administration had the ultimate idea: to buy us one by one (*laughter*). Not ministers, administrative cadre or political leaders but common citizens, by granting every American a permission —always with the Administration's prior consent, of course— to send remittances to Cubans even if they are not related.

I say: Very well, now we know we are worth something (*laughter*) since there are people willing to pay for us, a very rich government trying to buy us out. There are 4 billion poor in the world and they are not willing to pay a dime for any of them (*laughter and applause*). Our quotation in the market has been climbing.

I am telling you this because we are extending our medical care program to Suriname, which requested over 60 physicians. Even from a region in Canada, an autonomous province, its authorities requested physicians. They say: "We do not find physicians wanting to serve in the Arctic Circle. They do not want to come." We immediately told them: "Yes, but you discuss it with your government. It is up to you." Of course, conditions would be different, not because we would profit from it but because it is only logical for things to be different in case of an industrialized country. The physicians' services would be reasonably although modestly remunerated, since what moves us are not economic interests, but sincere wishes for international cooperation in the field of health, in which we have enough human resources.

If the Canadian official can overcome all the obstacles to take the physicians there, we will have Cuban doctors from the Amazonian jungle to the Arctic Circle (*applause*). But we are focused on the Third World. We pay our physicians their modest salaries in our country. It is good, we are all happy about that and our physicians are very happy with this arrangement, their morale is very high and they come from a great internationalist tradition.

We have received requests for cooperation from other places. Thus, the idea emerged of helping Haiti and later Central America. Now we see it is extending through Latin America and the Caribbean. We have no money, but we have human capital (*applause*).

You should not think I am boasting when I say that they would have to bring together all the physicians in the United States —I do not know how many they are— to try to find 2000 volunteers ready to go to the swamps, mountains and inhospitable places where our physicians go. It would be worthwhile to see what would happen, even though I know there are also altruistic physicians over there, that is for sure. But to find 2000 willing to leave the standard of living a consumer society offers and go to a swamp in Mosquito Coast, a place that not even the Spanish conquerors could stand, and that is really saying something (*laughter and applause*) that, perhaps, they may be unable to do. But Cuban physicians are there: that is human capital. If we take one out of every three physicians, we could offer the rest of Latin America the program we have offered Haiti and Central America, in places where similar conditions exist, where children and adults die for lack of medical care, in places no one else goes to. We have made the offer and it seems it will be accepted and our country will be in a position to respond. Such is the kind of human capital that can be created!

How many lives can be saved? We have suggested and publicly proclaimed the idea of having the countries in our region unite to save a million lives every year, including the lives of hundreds of thousands children. The cost of saving a million lives can be accurately estimated and saving the lives of children is the least costly, because older people need more laboratory tests and radiography, more medications and all that while children survive almost by themselves after the first year of life. At times a vaccine worth a few cents saves a life. Polio is a case in point.

We believe that a million lives can be saved every year with a small part of the money wasted in extravagant expenditures and there are physicians ready for the task. There may be more than enough medications in Europe but they will not save a million lives without the 15 000 to 20 000 physicians required to undertake a program such as this.

I am telling you about this so you know what Cuba is today, why Cuba is like that and what the prevailing standards are in Cuba, a country so miserably slandered in matters of human rights. A country where in forty years of Revolution there has never been a missing person, where there has never been a tortured person (*applause*), where there are no death squads and no political assassinations and nothing like that has ever happened. A country where there are no elderly people abandoned, no children living in the streets, without schools or teachers, no people left to their own lot.

We very well know what has happened in some of the places where our neighbors from the North have been, such as those who organized in 1954 the ousting of the government in one of the most important countries in the Central American region. They brought in their advisers with their handbooks on torture, repression and death. For many years there were no prisoners, this category did not exist, only dead and missing persons. A hundred thousand missing persons in just one country! And 50 thousand killed. We could add what happened in many other countries with tortures, murders, missing persons, repeated U.S. military interventions under any pretext or no pretext at all.

They do not remember that, they do not speak about that, they have lost their memory. In the light of the terrible experience undergone by the peoples of our America, we challenge them. We will demonstrate with actual facts, with realities, who has a humane sense of life, who has true humanitarian feelings and who is capable of doing something for mankind that is not lies, slogans, misinformation, hypocrisy, deception and all they have been doing in our region throughout this century (*applause*).

I know you do not need me to clarify all this to you but since I broached the subject I feel it is my duty to say so. It is very often that one meets misinformed persons who believe at least some of the tons of lies and slanders that have been cast against our country, in an attempt to hit us, to weaken us, to isolate us, to divide us. They have not been able to divide us and they won't be able to! (*applause*).

I have said all these things to you in the greatest intimacy. I could not come now and speak to you as I did in 1959 about organizing an expedition to solve a problem in a neighboring country (*laughter*). We very well know that today no country can solve its problems by itself. That is a reality in this globalized world. We can say here: "Either we are all saved or we all sink". (*Applause*.)

Martí said: "Humanity is my homeland." This is one of the most extraordinary things he said. That is how we have to think: Humanity is homeland!

I remember a case in Cuban history of a Spanish officer who during the Ten Years War —the first war for the independence of Cuba— when the Spanish government executed eight innocent medical students accused of desecrating the tomb of a rightist Spanish extremist, broke his sword in an imperishable gesture of indignation and protest and exclaimed: "Humanity comes before ones motherland" (*applause*). Of course, some parts of mankind are closer from home. When we think of mankind, the first thing that comes to our mind is our Latin American and Caribbean brothers and sisters, whom we never forget (*applause*). Then, comes the rest of that humanity on our planet. We will have to learn that concept, those principles contained in Martí's words —not only learn them, but feel them and practice them.

It is the Latin American countries'duty to unite without losing a single minute; the Africans are trying to do it. In Southeast Asia they have the ASEAN and are looking for other forms of economic integration. Europe is doing it at a swift pace. That is, there will be sub-regional and regional alliances in various parts of the world.

Bolívar dreamed of an extended regional federation from Mexico to Argentina. As you well know, the gentlemen from the North sabotaged the Amphictyonic Congress. They opposed Bolívar's idea of sending an expedition commanded by Sucre to liberate the island of Cuba and remove all risks of threat or counterattack by the fearful and tenacious Spanish metropolis; so we were not forgotten in Venezuelan history (*applause*). Now that we are free from the domination of a much stronger power, our most sacred duty is to defend our freedom for the very interest and security of our brothers and sisters in this hemisphere.

Obviously, we must work out various forms of cooperation and integration, step by step, but with swift steps if we want to survive as a regional entity with the same culture, the same language and so many things in common. This is something that Europe does not have. I do not know how an Italian understands an Austrian (*laughter*) or a Finn, how a German speaks with a Belgian or a Portuguese. But they have been able to create the European Union and they quickly advance towards a larger economic integration and a total monetary union. Why can we not be capable of at least considering this type of formulae? Why do we not encourage all the unitary and integrationist trends in every country sharing our language, our culture, our beliefs and the mixed blood running through the immense majority of us? And, where there is no mixed blood in our veins, there should be mixed blood in our souls (*applause*).

Who were those who fought in the Ayacucho battle? Men from the lowlands and from Caracas; Venezuelans from the West and the East, Colombians, Peruvians and Ecuadorians who were together and that is how they could do what they did. The unforgettable cooperation of Argentineans and Chileans was also present. Our greatest sin is that we lost, after almost 200 years.

Eleven years from now we will celebrate the 200th anniversary of the proclamation of the Venezuelan independence and later, in succession, that of the other countries. Almost two hundred years! What have we done in those 200 years, divided, fragmented, Balkanized, submitted as we have been? It is easier to control the seven dwarfs than to control a boxer, even he is a lightweight (*laughter*). They have wanted to keep us as divided neighboring dwarfs so they can control us.

I was discussing the need for unity not only in South America but in Central America and the Caribbean as well, and this is the moment to state it given what is happening in Venezuela. They have tried to divide us. The great power in the North wants FTAA and nothing more; a Free Trade Agreement and fast-track —I believe fast-track means quick, right? A quick step? Yes, I also recommend a fast-track for us, a fast-track to unite (*applause*). The Latin American answer to the fast-track from the North should be a fast-track from the Center and the South (*applause*).

Brazil should have our support and encouragement. We very well know that the United States does not like the existence of MERCOSUR, for it is an important embryo of an alliance that may become wider and grow. Some neighboring countries are not too far away from MERCOSUR. We see it as a sub-regional alliance, as a step toward a regional alliance, first of South America and then another step, as quick as possible, to embrace the Caribbean and Central America.

We are considering the need to advance in the contacts, the concept, the arrangements and the practical steps that may be taken in that direction before we can afford to consider the creation of a common currency. We believe that in that field the most we can do right now is to elaborate ideas and concepts. Meanwhile, we need to avoid, at all cost, the political and economic suicide of replacing our national currencies with the American currency, no matter the difficulties and fluctuations imposed by the present economic order. That would be tantamount to the annexation of Latin America to the United States. We would not be considered independent nations any more and we would be renouncing every possibility of taking part in the structuring of the future world. Under the present circumstances it is absolutely indispensable to unite, to come together and to expand our forces.

The meeting of the Caribbean Basin states will he held in the Dominican Republic on April. Later, almost immediately, there will be a meeting with the European Union in Rio de Janeiro. We have some common interests with the

Europeans; they are interested in some of our things and we are interested in some of theirs. Living under the slavery of only one currency, as we are now, is a tragedy and we are happy that with the euro, a rival to the Olympic champion, to the gold medal winner, has come into being (*laughter*).

The strengthening of the United Nations is another necessity that cannot be deferred. The United Nations must be democratized. The General Assembly, where all the member countries are represented, should be granted the highest authority, as well as the functions and role befitting it. The Security Council's dictatorship must end together with the dictatorship the United States exercises within that body (*applause*).

If the veto power cannot be eliminated because those who have the last word about such a reform are precisely those with the power to veto it, we strongly demand that the privilege be at least shared. The number of permanent members must be suitably increased from the five they are now in compliance with the growth of the UN membership and the great changes that have taken place in fifty years. The Third World, where a great number of countries emerged as independent States after World War II, should have the possibility to share equal prerogatives in that important United Nations body. We have defended the idea of having two representatives for Latin America and the Caribbean basin, two for Africa and two for the underdeveloped regions in Asia, as a minimum. If two are not enough, the figure could be risen to three, in one or more of the above mentioned regions. We constitute the immense majority at the United Nations General Assembly and cannot continue being ignored.

We would not oppose the admission of other industrialized countries but we give absolute priority to the presence of permanent representatives of Latin America and the Caribbean and the other above mentioned regions in the Security Council, with the same prerogatives of its other permanent members (*applause*). If it is not so, we will have three categories of members: permanent members with veto power, permanent members without veto power and non-permanent members. And there is still more of this madness. Aimed at dividing and thus preserving the privileges of their present status, at the same time it reduces the prerogatives of the potential new permanent members, the United States has come up with the idea of rotating that condition among two or more countries from the various regions; that is, to reduce this vital reform to zero, to nothing, to simple salt and water.

There is another way to regulate the irritating veto prerogative with an increase in the number of members needed to apply it, that is, the General Assembly may be given the possibility of taking part in the main decisions. Would not this be more democratic and fair?

A battle must be waged there. All the Third World countries should unite. We say that to Africans when we meet with them, also to Asians, to the Caribbeans, to everyone in every international agency: the United Nations, the Non-Aligned Countries Movement, the Lome meetings, the Group of 77, everywhere. We are a large number of countries sharing common interests, wishing to advance and develop; we are the overwhelming majority in almost all international institutions and you may rest assured that we are advancing in building an awareness about the fate reserved to us. We must work, persuade, fight and persevere. We must never be discouraged.

Those in the North are constantly scheming to divide us. I am going to give you four examples having to do with Latin America.

They do not like MERCOSUR that has already achieved some measure of economic success even though it is but an embryo of the great regional integration we hope for, and they do not want at all. What is it they devise? Well, many things. First, they organize those hemispheric meetings leaving out Cuba, a reaction to the first Ibero-American Summit in Guadalajara.

They devise the idea of having only one Latin American permanent member in the Security Council, to have several important members of our region confronting each other. They immediately add the advisability of rotating the position among Brazil, Argentina and Mexico, of course, with no veto power. Then, they create the special category of strategic ally for Argentina. That plants distrust and restlessness among important fraternal neighbors that should closely unite and cooperate, particularly now when MERCOSUR is advancing.

They invent the Machiavellian decision of releasing the sale of sophisticated arms to countries in the region, which may unleash a costly, destructive and fissiparous arms race among them. Why arms when there is neither a Cold War nor the ghost of the Soviet Union or any other foreign threat to security but that coming from the United States itself? Can these arms contribute to the unity, cooperation, integration, progress and peace among us? What do we need to open up our eyes and finally understand the geo-strategic purposes of this policy?

They have not been able to continue leaving our small country out everywhere. We already take part in the Ibero-American Summits. We are members of the Association of Caribbean States. We belong to the Latin American Economic System and have been included in the Latin American Integration Association. We maintain excellent relations with the Caribbean Community (CARICOM). We will be present in the important Summit of the European Union, Latin America and the Caribbean to be held in Rio de Janeiro. We have been admitted as observers among the countries in the Lome Convention. We are active members of the Group of 77 and hold an outstanding place as founding members of the Non-Aligned Movement. We belong to the WTO and are very present at the United Nations, which is a great forum and an institution that, once democratized, may become a basic pillar for a fair and humane globalization.

What are we doing there? Talking, explaining, submitting problems that we know touch a large part of mankind very dearly because we are free to do it. There are brotherly countries in Africa, Asia, Latin America and other places that would like to submit many things with much energy but do not have the same possibilities

Cuba has. Being already excluded from all international financial institutions, blockaded and submitted to an economic warfare, invulnerable to any retaliation of that type, strengthened by forty years of hard long struggle which gives us an absolute liberty to do anything, Cuba can speak up. They may be in crucial need of a credit from the World Bank or from the Inter-American Bank or from another regional bank, or of some negotiation with the International Monetary Fund, or of an export credit, which is one of the many mechanisms used by the United States to limit their possibilities of action. That is why quite often Cuba has taken upon itself such task.

In spite of everything, there are people in our impoverished world who are so courageous that, for example, at the United Nations, the Cuban motion against the blockade received the support of 157 votes against 2 (*applause*). We had spent seven years in this exercise. The first time there were some 55 votes in favor and four or five against and all the rest, abstentions or absences. Who could want to be at odds with the Yankees? Because voting there is by show of hands (*laughter*).

But people lose fear and fear was gradually lost; dignity may grow and it does. The following year, there were more than sixty, then more than seventy, then over a hundred. Now, after we have the support of almost 160 countries and only two are against, it can hardly grow anymore. In the end, there will be no country supporting this inhuman, cruel and unlimited action except the United States, unless a day comes when the United States votes for us and supports the Cuban motion (*laughter and applause*).

We are making progress, gaining ground. The peoples know, intuitively or instinctively, that we are very often slandered. The peoples have a great instinct! Besides, the peoples know them because they are everywhere doing all sorts of things, abusing people and sowing selfishness and hatred. People know them. Contempt is difficult to hide and the Third World countries suffer under such arrogance and contempt.

The various US administrations with their blockade, their constant harassment and their exclusions have given us the possibility of fighting them in full and of being even joyful to be excluded in exchange for the freedom to speak without compromise in any forum of the world where there are so many fair causes to defend (*applause*).

For the reasons I have already explained we may have some sympathies with other countries. As for them, who are the main stronghold of reaction and injustice in our times, we can say the truth and always the truth, with and without relations, with and without a blockade. They should entertain no illusions that, if some day they lift the blockade, Cuba will stop speaking as frankly and honestly as it has done for forty years! (*applause and comments*). It is a historic duty.

I will finish in a minute, if you allow me. (*Voices: "No!"*) Remember I am a visitor here (*laughter*) and I am here before you, before the university students. I am in this country that I sincerely admire and deeply love (*applause*). I am not flattering you. I was always very fond of history. The first thing I studied was precisely history because when I began the first grade they immediately handed me a book on sacred history where I learned some things I still remember (*laughter*). Of course, I learned about the history of the Arc, the Exodus, the battles and the crossing of the Red Sea. At times, when I speak with some rabbi friends and I ask them: "Tell me the truth, where did you turn?" (*Laughter.*) In jest, because I really respect religions and I have considered it an elementary duty to respect the beliefs of every individual.

At times I discuss even theological issues about the world, the universe. When the Pope visited Cuba, I had the satisfaction and the opportunity of meeting some very intelligent theologians whom I bombed with every type of questions (*laughter and applause*). I did not dare ask any of them about dogma or matters of faith but I did ask other types of questions about space, universe, the theories about its origin, the possibilities of there being life on other planets and things that can be very seriously dealt with. With seriousness and respect you can talk about any topic, and based on that respect ask questions and at times even make jokes.

Well, here I am and I was going to tell you that I should say something about Venezuela, right? If you allow me to. (*Applause and exclamations of: "Yes!"*) You are going to say: "He came to Venezuela and did not say anything about us." Let me warn you that this is not an easy task, for the reasons I have already explained.

I began telling you that it is a country I love dearly. This is when I began to tell you about my love for history, for universal history, for the history of revolutions and wars, for the history of Cuba, the history of Latin America, and especially for that of Venezuela. That is why I identified myself so much with Bolívar's life and ideas.

Fate would have it that Venezuela should be the country to fight the most for the independence of this hemisphere (*applause*). It began here and you had a legendary precursor like Miranda, who even lead a French army in campaign waging famous battles which, at a point in time, during the French Revolution, prevented an invasion of French territory. He had also fought in the United States for that countrys independence. I have a wide collection of books about Miranda's great life, although I have not been able to read them all. The Venezuelans, therefore, had Miranda, the forefather of Latin America's independence, and later Bolívar, the Liberator, who was always for me the greatest among the greatest men in history. (From the audience they shout: "Fidel too!")

Please, put me in the forty-thousandth place. I always remember one of Martí's phrases deeply engraved in my mind: "All the glory in the world can fit into a kernel of corn." Many great people in history were concerned about glory and that is no reason to criticize them. Perhaps it was the concept of time, the sense of history, the future, the importance and survival of events in their lives what they took for glory. This is natural and understandable. Bolívar liked to speak about glory and he spoke very strongly about glory. He cannot be criticized; a great aura of glory will forever be attached to his name.

Martí's concept, which I entirely share, associates glory to personal vanity and self-exaltation. The role of the individual in important historic events has been very much debated and even admitted. What I especially like about Martí's phrase is the idea of man's insignificance as compared to the enormous significance and transcendence of humanity and the immeasurable reach of universe, the reality that we are really like a small speck of dust floating in space. However, that reality does not diminish man's greatness a single bit. On the contrary, it is enhanced when, like in Bolívar's case, he carried in his mind a whole universe full of just ideas and noble sentiments. That is why I admire Bolívar so much. That is why I consider his work so immense. He does not belong to the stock of men who conquered territories and nations, or founded empires that gave fame to others; he created nations, freed territories and tore empires. He was also a brilliant soldier, a distinguished thinker and prophet.

Today, we are trying to do what he wanted to do and remains to be done. We are trying to unite our peoples so that tomorrow, following the same train of unitary thought, the only one which corresponds with our specie and our age, human beings will be able to know and live in a united, brotherly, just and free world. That is what he wanted to do with the white, black, native and mixed peoples of our America.

Here we are in this land for which we feel special admiration, respect and love. When I came 40 years ago, I expressed it with deep gratitude because nowhere else was I better received, with so much affection and enthusiasm. The only thing I could be ashamed of is that I was actually in kindergarten when that first meeting in this prestigious university was held (*laughter and applause*).

Having said this, I will now express, as briefly as possible, the reflection I wanted to make about Venezuela. I am sure not all of you will agree with it. The idea is to make and honest, calmed and objective analysis.

Figures and data this visitor has tried to analyze lead him to the conclusion that in this new dawn the people of Venezuela will have to face courageously and intelligently serious difficulties arising from the current economic situation.

Commodity exports according to Central Bank report:

In 1997: 23.4 billion dollars (services, which have almost balanced expenditures and income, are not included here).

In 1998: 17.32 billions. In other words, the value of exports dropped by 6.080 million dollars in only one year.

Oil (the main export item) Prices: 1996: around 20 USD per barrel; 1997: 16.50 USD; 1998: around 9 USD.

The basic minerals: iron, aluminum, gold and by-products like steel, have all, to a greater or lesser degree, significantly dropped in price. Both items make up 77% of exports. I mean, oil and minerals.

Favorable balance of trade:

1996- 13.6 billion dollars

1998- 3.4 billions

Difference: 10.2 billions in just 2 years

Balance of payment:

1996- 7 billions favorable to Venezuela

1998- 3.42 billions unfavorable to the country

Difference: more than 10 billions.

International reserves available:

In 1997: 17.818 millions

In 1998: 14.385 million dollars

Net losses: approximately 3.5 billions in one year

Foreign debt:

In 1998: 31.6 billions, not including the private short-term financial debt. Almost 40% of the country's budget are spent servicing the foreign debt.

Social situation according to different national and international sources literally ratified yesterday by President Chávez (*applause*):

Unemployment, he said: Official figures report 11% to 12%. Other figures indicate 20%.

Underemployment (which supposedly includes unemployment) —the parenthetical expression is mine— is around 50%.

Almost a million children in a *state of survival* —his own terms.

Infant mortality is almost 28 per 1000 live births. 15% of those deaths are due to malnutrition.

Deficit in housing: 1.5 millions.

Only one in 5 children completes grammar school; 45% of adolescents do not attend secondary school.

If you allow me, I will give you an example: 95% of children of that age are in secondary school in Cuba. That is almost as high as you can go. I say this because 45% children out of school are really an impressive figure.

To these data given by the President in his tight synthesis, we could add others taken from various, reliable sources.

More than a million children are in the labor market; over 2.3 millions, who are out of the school system, have no trade whatsoever.

In the last ten years, more than a million Venezuelans who belonged to the middle class "c" category —as you can see, there are also categories within the middle class-fell to the category of poor and destitute amounting today to 77% of the population. This is due to a drop in incomes, unemployment and the effects of inflation. This means that categories "c", "d" and "e" include today from the poor to the destitute.

This was occurring, as President Chávez said with meaningful and bitter words, in Bolívar's original homeland, the country in the Americas which is the richest in natural resources, has almost one million square kilometers and a population of no more than 22 millions.

I am trying to meditate with you here.

I must say, first and foremost, that I am a friend of Chávez's (*applause*), but no one asked me to address any special issue. No official in his team, no Venezuelan politician or friend knew absolutely anything about what I was going to talk about this afternoon here, in such an important and strategic place as the Central University of Venezuela. I am offering this reflections under my total and absolute responsibility in the hope that they can be useful.

What are we worried about? I seem to perceive at this moment an exceptional situation in the history of Venezuela. I have witness two unique moments: first that moment in January 1959, and forty years later, I have seen the extraordinary volatility of the people on February 2, 1999. I have seen a people reborn. A people such as I saw in Plaza del Silencio (Silence Square) where I was a bit more silent than I have been here... (*Laughter.*) I even had to reply to an excellent citizen of Caracas, because in fulfilling my elementary duty as a visitor, I mentioned a few personalities that were in the government, beginning with Admiral Larrazábal, and when I mentioned another important political personality of the time, there was noise, protests, which, in turn, made me protest. I complained because that really embarrassed me. I think I even blushed. I told them: "I am not mentioning names here for you to boo." I expressed my complaint to the multitude gathered there at Plaza del Silencio. Those were unquestionably revolutionary masses.

It was once again very impressive to see the people in such extraordinary high spirits although under different circumstances. Back then, hopes had been left behind. I do not want to explain why; I leave that to the historians. This time hope lies ahead. I see in these hopes a true rebirth of Venezuela, or at least an exceptionally great opportunity for Venezuela. I see it coming not only in the interest of the Venezuelans, I also see it in the interest of Latin Americans. I see it as something in the interest of other peoples in the world, as it advances —because there is no other choice— towards a universal globalization.

There is no way of escaping it, and there is no alternative. So I am not trying to flatter you with my words. I rather remind you of your duty, the duty of the nation, of the people, of all those who were born after that visit, of the youngest, of the more mature, who really have a great responsibility ahead of you. I think opportunities have often been lost, but you would not be forgiven if you lose this one (*applause*).

The person speaking to you here has had the privilege and the opportunity of accumulating some political experience, of having lived through a revolutionary process in a country where, as I have already said, people did not even want to hear about socialism. And when I say people, I mean the vast majority. That same majority supported the Revolution, supported the leaders, supported the Rebel Army but there were ghosts they were afraid of. What Pavlov did with his famous dogs, it is the same thing the United States did with many of us and who knows with how many millions of Latin Americans: create conditioned reflexes in us.

We have had to fight a lot against scarcity and poverty. We have had to learn to do a lot with little. We had good and bad moments, the former especially when we were able to establish trade agreements with the socialist block and the Soviet Union and demanded fairer prices for our export products. Because we observed how the prices of what they exported rose while those of our products, in the course of a five-year trade agreement, remained the same. Then, at the end of the five-year period, we had less purchasing power. We proposed a sliding clause: when the prices of the products that they exported to us rose, the prices of the products that we exported to them also automatically rose. We resorted to diplomacy, to the doctrine and the eloquence that revolutionaries in a country that had to overcome so many obstacles must have.

Actually, the Soviets felt great sympathy for Cuba and great admiration for our Revolution. It was very surprising for them to see that after so many years a tiny country, right next to the United States, would rebel against that mighty superpower. They had never contemplated such possibility and they would have never advised it to anyone. Luckily we never asked anybody for advise (*laughter*), although we had already read almost a whole library of the works of Marx, Engels, Lenin and other theoreticians. We were convinced Marxists and socialists.

With that fever and that blind passion that characterizes young people, and sometimes old people too (*applause*). I assumed the basic principles that I learned from those books and they helped me understand the society where I lived. Until then it was for me an intricate entanglement for which I could not find any convincing explanation. I must say that the famous *Communist Manifesto*, which Marx and Engels took so long to write —you can tell that its main author worked conscientiously, a phrase he liked to use, and must have revised it more times than Balzac revised each page of any of his novels— impressed me tremendously because for the first time in my life I realized a few truths that I had never seen before.

Before that, I was a sort of utopian communist. I began to draw my own conclusions and ended up being a utopian communist while studying from an enormous book with some 900 mimeographed pages, the first political economy course they taught us in Law School. It was a political economy inspired in the ideas of capitalism but which mentioned and analyzed very briefly the different schools and criteria. Later, in the second course, I paid much attention to the subject and meditated on the basis of rational viewpoints, so I ended up being a utopian communist. I call it that because my doctrine had no scientific or historic basis whatsoever. It was based on the good wishes of a student recently graduated from a Jesuit's school. And I am very grateful because they taught me some things that have helped me in life, above all, to have strength, a certain sense of honor and definite ethical principles that these Spanish Jesuits although very distant from any of the ideas I uphold today instilled in their pupils.

I came out of that school an athlete, an explorer and a mountain climber. I entered the University of Havana ignorant about politics, without a revolutionary private tutor who would have been so useful to me at that stage of my life.

That is how I came to have my own ideas, which I preserve and maintain with growing loyalty and fervor. Maybe it is because I now have a little more experience and knowledge, and maybe also because I have had the opportunity of meditating about new problems that did not even exist during Marx's time.

For example, the word *environment* was probably never pronounced by anyone in all of Karl Marx's life, except Malthus who said that the population grew in geometric progression and that there would not be enough food for so many people. He thus became a sort of forerunner of today's ecologists, although he maintained ideas concerning the economy and salaries we cannot but disagree with (*laughter*).

So I am wearing the same coat I wore when I came to this university 40 years ago (*applause*), the same one I wore when I attacked the Moncada garrison, when we disembarked from *Granma* (*applause*). I would venture to say, despite the many pages of adventure that anyone can find in my revolutionary life, that I always tried to be wise and sensible, although perhaps I have been wiser than sensible.

In our conception and development of the Cuban Revolution, we acted as Martí said when, on the eve of his death in combat, he addressed the great anti-imperialist objective of his struggle: "It had to be in silence and sort of indirectly since the achievement of certain goals demands concealment for, if proclaimed for what they really are, obstacles so formidable would rise as to prevent their attainment."

I was discreet, but not as much as I should have been because I would explain Marx's ideas and the class society to everyone I met. So, in the people's movement whose slogan in its fight against corruption was "Dignity against Money" which I had joined as soon as I arrived at the university, they were beginning to take me for a communist. Towards the end of my university studies, I was no longer a utopian communist but rather an atypical communist who was acting freely. I based myself in a realistic analysis of our country's situation.

Those were the times of McCarthyism and Cuba's Marxist Party, the People's Socialist Party was almost completely isolated. However, within the movement I had joined, which had now become the Cuban People's Party, a large mass, in my opinion, had a class instinct but lacked a class consciousness: peasants, workers, professionals, middle-class people, good, honest, potentially revolutionary people. Its founder and leader, a man of great charisma, had dramatically taken his own life a few months before the 1952 coup d'état. The younger ranks of that party later became an important part of our movement.

I was a member of that political organization which, as it usually happened, was already falling into the hands of rich people, and I knew by heart what was going to happen after the then inevitable electoral triumph. But I had come up with some ideas, also on my own —just imagine the things a utopian can think up— about what had to be done in Cuba and how to do it, despite the United States. Those masses had to be led along a revolutionary path. Maybe that was the merit of the tactic we pursued. Of course, we were reading Marx's, Engels's and Lenin's books.

When we attacked the Moncada garrison we left one of Lenins books behind, and the first thing the propaganda of Batista's regime said during the trial was that it was a conspiracy of corrupt members of the recently overthrown government, bankrolled with their money, and communist too. No one knows how both categories could be reconciled.

In the trial, I assumed my own defense. It was not that I thought myself a good lawyer but I thought that I was the person who could best defend myself at that moment. I put on a gown and took my place with the lawyers. It was a political and not a penal trial. I did not intend to be acquitted but to disseminate ideas. I began to cross-examine all those killers who had murdered dozens upon dozens of our comrades and were there as witnesses; I turned the trial against them (*applause*). So the next day they took me out of there, they put me away and declared me ill (*laughter*).

That was the last thing they did although they really wanted to do away with me once and for all; but, well, I knew very well why they checked themselves. I knew and I know the psychology of all of those people. It was due to the mood and the situation with the people, the rejection and huge indignation caused by all the murders they had committed. I also had a bit of luck. But the fact is that at the beginning, while they were questioning me, this book of Lenin appears. Someone takes it out and says: "You people had a book of Lenin."

We were explaining who we were: Martí followers, that was the truth, that we had nothing to do with that corrupt government that they had ousted from power, that our objectives were such and such. However, we did not say a word about Marxism-Leninism, neither did we have to. We said what we had to say but since the subject of the book came up at the trial, I felt really irritated and said: "Yes, that book by Lenin is ours, we read Lenin's books and other socialist books, and whoever does not read them is an ignorant." That is what I told the judges and the rest of the people there (*applause*). That was insufferable. We were not going to say: "Listen, that little book was planted there by somebody..." (*Laughter.*)

Our program had been presented when I defended myself at the trial, therefore, those who did not know how we thought was because they did not want to know. Perhaps they tried to ignore that speech known as *History Will Absolve Me* with which I defended myself all alone over there. Because, as I have explained, I was expelled, they declared me ill, they tried all the others and sent me to a hospital to try me, in a small ward. They did not exactly hospitalize me but put me in an isolated prison cell. In the hospital, they turned a small ward into a courtroom with the judges and a few other people crammed into it, most of them from the military. They tried me there, and I had the pleasure of saying there all that I thought, everything, quite defiantly.

I wonder why they were not able to deduce what our political thought was, for it was all there. It contained you might say the foundation of a socialist government program although we were convinced the time was not ripe, that the right time and stages would come. That was when we spoke about the land reform among many other things of a social and economic nature. We said that all the profits obtained by all those gentlemen with so much money —that is, the surplus value but without using such terminology— (*laughter*) should be used for the development of the country, and I hinted that it was the government's responsibility to look after the development of the country and that surplus money.

I even spoke about the golden calf. I recalled the Bible once again and singled out "those who worshipped the golden calf", in a clear reference to those who expected everything from capitalism. Those were elements enough for them to deduce our way of thinking.

Later, I have meditated that it is likely that many of those who could be affected by a true revolution did not believe us at all, because in the 57 years of Yankee neocolonialism, many a progressive or revolutionary program had been proclaimed. The ruling classes never believed our program to be possible or permissible by the United States. They did not pay much attention to it. They heeded it and even found it funny. At the end of the day, all the programs used to be abandoned and people would become corrupt. So they probably said: "Yes, the illusions of these romantic young men are very pretty, very nice, but, why worry about that?"

They did not like Batista. They admired the frontal fight against his abusive and corrupt regime and they possibly underestimated the thoughts contained in that declaration, which were the basis of what we later did and of what we think today. The difference is that many years of experience have further enriched our knowledge and perceptions about all those problems. So, as I have said, that is the way I have thought since then.

We have undergone the tough experience of a long revolutionary period, especially during the last ten years, confronting extremely powerful forces under very difficult circumstances. Well, I will tell you the truth: we achieved what seemed impossible. I would venture to say that near miracles were performed. Of course, the laws were passed exactly as they had been promised always with United States angry and arrogant opposition. It had had great influence in our country, so it made itself felt and the process became increasingly radicalized with each blow and aggression we suffered.

Thus began the long struggle we have waged until today. The forces in our country polarized. Fortunately, the vast majority was in favor of the Revolution and a minority, around 10% or less, was against it. So there has always been a great consensus and a great support for all that process until today. One knows what to worry about, because we made a great effort to overcome the prejudices that existed, to convey ideas, to build a consciousness and it was not an easy work.

I remember the first time I spoke about racial discrimination. I had to go on television about three times. I was surprised at how deeply rooted, more than we had supposed, had become the prejudices brought to us by our northern neighbors: that certain clubs were for white people only and the rest could not go there, as well as certain beaches. Almost all the beaches, especially in the capital, were exclusively for whites. There were even segregated parks and promenades, where according to the color of your skin you had to walk in one direction or another. What we did was to open all the beaches for all of the people and from the very first days we prohibited discrimination in all places of recreation, parks and promenades. That humiliating injustice was incompatible with the Revolution.

One day I spoke and I explained these things. There was such reaction, such rumors and so many lies! They said we were going to force white men into marrying black women and white women into marrying black men. Well, just like that other preposterous invention that we were going to deprive families of the parental custody of their children. I once again had to go on television on the subject of discrimination to reply to all those rumors and machinations and explain the matter once again. That phenomenon, which was nothing but an imposed racist culture, a humiliating, cruel prejudice was very hard to eradicate.

In other words, during those years, we devoted a great deal of our time to two things: defending ourselves from expeditions, threats of foreign aggression, dirty war, assassination attempts, sabotages, etc. and building consciousness. There was a moment when there were armed mercenary bands in every province of our country, promoted and supplied by the United States. But we confronted them immediately, we gave them no time. They had not the slightest chance to prosper because our own experience in irregular warfare was very recent and we were practically one of the few revolutionary countries which totally defeated these bands despite the logistic support they received from abroad. We had to devote a lot of our time to that.

One problem I see, one source of concern I have is that many expectations have been raised in Venezuela by the extraordinary results of the elections, and it is logical. What do I mean? I mean the natural, logical tendency of the people to dream, to wish that a great number of accumulated problems be solved in a matter of months. As an honest friend of yours, in my own opinion, I think there are problems here that will not be solved in months, or years (*applause*).

That is why I read the data. Because we are daily looking at and analyzing similar data in our country: the price of nickel or sugar; the yield of a hectare of sugar cane; if there is a drought, if there is not; how much income we are getting; how much we owe; what must be purchased urgently; what the prices of powdered milk, cereals, indispensable medicines, inputs for production and all the other things are and what it is to be done.

At a given point in time our sugar production was boosted, almost doubled. There were good prices, we purchased machinery and began to build the infrastructure. Investments in industry and agriculture increased, limited only by Soviet technological resources, which were more advanced in some fields and less advanced in others. They generally consumed too much fuel.

But we bought all the steel we needed that was not covered by our national production. Half a million cubic meters of timber arrived in Cuba from Siberia every year, purchased with sugar, nickel and other products that, thanks to the sliding prices —the agreement we had reached before the oil prices surge— increased their prices as the price of oil increased (*applause*). And do you know how much we got to consume? Thirteen million tons a year. Not only due to all the transportation services, the mechanization of agriculture and port facilities, the construction of tens of thousands of kilometers of highway, hundreds of big and small dams, mainly for agriculture, houses, dairy farms, all equipped with milking machines, thousands of schools and other social facilities but also because of the power consumption in industries and homes. The electrification of the country benefited 95% of the population. There were resources but I could add that we were not even able to manage them with maximum efficiency.

Now we do, we have learned. In times of abundance, you do not learn much, but in times of scarcity, real scarcity, you learn quite a lot. But we did all those things that allowed us to achieve these results in the economic, social and other spheres I have talked about.

Our country also holds first place in education, in teachers per capita. Recently, UNESCO issued a very rewarding report. A survey was conducted among 54,000 children in the third and fourth grade of grammar school about their knowledge of mathematics and language, in 14 Latin American countries, among the most advanced. An average was obtained: some were above the average and others were below but Cuba ranked first by a wide margin, almost twice the average of the rest of Latin America (*applause*). In all the parameters, such as student's age per grade, retention rate, non-repeating students and other factors which measure the quality of grammar school, we hold, without exception, the place of honor, placing our country, all by itself, in category 1.

There are a large number of new teachers and every passing year they accumulate more knowledge and experience, just like there is a large number of doctors who gather more and more knowledge with each passing year. The same thing happens with professionals in general and several fields in particular. The percentage of the gross income that we invest in science is incomparably higher than that of the most advanced countries in Latin America, with tens of thousands of scientific workers, many of them with postgraduate degrees and constantly raising their knowledge. We have done a lot of things and invested mainly in human capital.

What do I fear? It is this, which I frankly say here and I am willing to say anywhere. You people lived through periods of abundance (*they tell him that very long ago*) okay, long ago. In 1972 the price of oil was 1.90 USD a barrel. For example, at the triumph of the Revolution, Cuba could buy the 4 million tons of fuel it consumed with a few hundred thousand tons of sugar, at the normal world sugar price existing then. When the price of fuel suddenly rose we were saved by the already mentioned sliding price. But when the crisis came —after the USSR was lost and our basic market with it, as well as all our agreed prices— we had to cut by half the 13 million tons of oil which was our consumption by then. A large part of what we were exporting we had to invest in fuel, and we learned to save.

I have already talked about baseball players. I would add that in every small village there were baseball players and they would use tractors and wagons to transport the players and fans to the games. And there were even some tractor drivers who used them to go visit their sweethearts (*laughter*). We had gone from 5 000 tractors to 80 000.

The people owned everything. We had changed the system but we had not learned much about management and control. We also made some idealistic mistakes. But we had a lot more things to distribute than what we have today. Some said that Cuba had "socialized poverty". We answered, "Yes, it is better to socialize poverty than to distribute the scarce wealth there is among a small minority that takes everything and leaves nothing for the rest of the people."

Now more than ever, we are forced to distribute what we have as equitably as possible. However, there are now some privileges in our country. The reasons were inevitable for us: family remittances, tourism, opening to foreign investment in certain branches of the economy, something which has made our work in the political and ideological field more difficult, because the power of money is great; it must not be underestimated.

We have had to struggle a lot against all that. On the other hand, we had reached the conclusion that living in a glass case might be very pure but those who live that way, in total aseptic conditions, when they are out of them they may be finished off by a mosquito, an insect, a bacteria, just like many of the bacteria, parasites and viruses that the Spaniards brought over with them killed a great number of natives in this hemisphere. They lacked immunity. We said, "We will learn to work under difficult conditions because, at the end of the day, virtue flourishes in the fight against vice." Thus, we have had to face many problems under the present circumstances.

You had a period of huge incomes when the price of oil rose from 1.90 USD a barrel in 1972; to 10.41 USD in 1974; to 13.03 USD in 1978; to 29.75 USD in 1979; until reaching the fabulous price of 35.69 USD in 1980. In the following years, from 1981 to 1985, the average price per barrel was 30.10 USD, a true stream of income in convertible currencies for this item. I know the story of what happened later, because I have a lot of friends who are professionals and every time I saw them I would ask about the situation, what was their salary then and what was their real income 10 years later. I have witnessed how that income dwindled year after year until today. I should not really make any other type of analysis. I always asked the Venezuelans those questions thinking about the country's situation.

These are not times of abundance neither for Venezuela nor for the world. I am fulfilling an honest duty, a friend's duty, a brother's duty, by suggesting to you, who are a powerful intellectual vanguard, to meditate profoundly about these topics. We want to express to you our concern that this logical, natural and human hope, stemming from a sort of political miracle that has taken place in Venezuela might, in a short term, turn into disappointment and a weakening of such an extraordinary process (*applause*).

I ask myself, I should and I do: What economic feats or miracles may be expected immediately with the prices of Venezuelan export commodities so low and oil at 9 USD a barrel? What with the lowest price in the last 25 years, a dollar which has a lot less purchasing power now, with a larger population, an enormous accumulation of social problems, an international economic crisis and a neo-liberally globalized world?

I cannot and should not say a word as to what we would do under such circumstances. I cannot. I am here as a guest, not as an adviser, an opinion giver or anything like that. I am simply meditating.

Allow me to say that I do not want to mention any but there are some important countries whose situation is worse than yours, which I hope can overcome their difficulties.

Your situation is difficult, but not catastrophic. That would be our perception if we were in your place. I will tell you more with the same frankness. You cannot do what we did in 1959. You will have to be more patient than we were, and I am referring to that part of the people who want radical economic and social changes in the country.

If the Cuban Revolution had triumphed in a moment such as this, it would not have been able to sustain itself, I mean that same Cuban Revolution which has done all it has done. It emerged —and not because it was so calculated, but by a rare historic coincidence— 14 years after the Second World War, in a bipolar world. We did not know a single Soviet citizen, nor did we ever receive a single bullet from the Soviets to carry out our struggle and our Revolution. Neither did we let ourselves to be guided by any type of political advice after the triumph, nor did anybody ever attempt it because we were very reluctant to that. We, Latin Americans in particular, do not like to be told what to do.

At that moment, of course, there was another powerful pole and so we anchored ourselves to that pole, which had come out of a great social revolution. It helped us to face the monster that cut off its oil and other vital supplies and reduced its imports of Cuban sugar bringing them down to zero as soon as we enforced a land reform law. Therefore, from one minute to the next, we were deprived of a market that had taken more than a century to build.

The Soviets, on the other hand, sold us oil. At world price, yes; to be paid in sugar, yes; at the world price of sugar, yes, but we exported our sugar to the USSR and we received oil, raw materials, food, and many other things. It gave us time to build a consciousness; it gave us time to sow ideas; it gave us time to create a new political culture (*applause*). It gave us time! Enough time to build the strength that enabled us later to resist the most incredibly hard times.

All the internationalism that we have practiced, which has already been mentioned, also made us stronger.

I do not think any country has endured more difficult circumstances. I am not at all boastful if I tell you, objectively, that no country in the world could have resisted. There might be some. If I think of the Vietnamese, I think the Vietnamese capable of any kind of resistance (*applause*). I think of the Chinese were equally capable of performing any kind of feat.

There are people with peculiar characteristics and conditions, deeply rooted cultures all their own, inherited from age-old ancestors, which give them enormous capacity for resistance. In the case of Cuba, it was a culture largely inherited from a world that became our enemy. We were completely surrounded by hostile regimes, hostile campaigns, a blockade and all sorts of economic pressures, which made our revolutionary tasks extremely difficult. We spent six years in war against the bandits employed by our powerful neighbor to implement its dirty war tactics. Also, many years fighting terrorists, assassination attempts... what else can I say, if not that it is a great privilege for me, after 40 years, to return to this place, so dear and unforgettable to me already (*applause*). This is evidence of the inefficiency and failure of those who so often tried to accelerate the natural and inevitable process of life toward the end.

Now we can say the same thing a lieutenant said who took me prisoner in a forest near Santiago de Cuba in the early hours of dawn several days after the attack against the Moncada army garrison. We had made a mistake, there is always a mistake. We were tired of sleeping on the ground, over roots and stones, so we fell asleep in a makeshift hut covered with palm fronds. Then, we woke up with rifles pointed against our chests. It was a lieutenant, a black man, with a group of unmistakably bloodthirsty soldiers who did not know who we were. We had not been identified. At first, they did not identify us. They asked us our names. I gave a false name. Prudence, huh? (*Laughter.*) Shrewdness? (*Applause.*) Perhaps it was intuition or maybe instinct. I can assure you that I was not afraid because there are moments in life when it is so, when you consider yourself as good as dead, and then it is rather your honor, your pride, your dignity that reacts.

If I had given them my name, that would have been it: tah, tah, tah! They would have done away with that small group immediately. A few minutes later they found some weapons nearby. These had been left behind by some comrades who were not in physical conditions to continue the struggle. Some of them were wounded and we had all agreed they should return to the city to turn themselves in to the judicial authorities. Only three of us were stayed, only three armed comrades! And we were captured the way I have just explained.

But that lieutenant, what an incredible thing! I have never told this story in detail publicly. This lieutenant was trying to calm down the soldiers but he could hardly stop them anymore. When they found the other comrades' weapons while searching the surroundings, they were infuriated. They had us tied up with their loaded rifles pointing at us. But the lieutenant moved around calming them down and repeating in a low voice: "You cannot kill ideas, you cannot kill ideas." What made this man say that?

He was a middle-aged man. He had taken some university courses and he had that idea in his head, and he felt the urge to express it in a low voice, as if talking to himself: "You cannot kill ideas." Well, when I look at this man and I see his attitude, in a critical moment when he was hardly able to keep those angry soldiers from firing, I get up and tell him: "Lieutenant", him alone, of course, "I am so and so, first in command of the action. Seeing your chivalrous attitude, I cannot deceive you, I want you to know who you have taken prisoner." And the man says, "Do not tell anyone! Do not tell anyone!" (*Applause.*) I applaud that man because he saved my life three times in a few hours.

A few minutes later they were taking us with them and the soldiers were still very irritated. They heard some shots not far from there, got ready for combat and said to us, "Drop down to the ground." I remained standing and I said, "I will not drop to the ground!" I thought it was some kind of trick to eliminate us, and I said, "No." I also told the lieutenant who kept insisting that we protected ourselves, "I am not dropping to the ground, if they want to shoot let them shoot." Then he says, listen to what he says, "You boys are very brave." What an incredible reaction!

I do not mean that he saved my life at that moment, but he had that gesture. After we reached a road, he put us in a truck and there was a major there who was very bloodthirsty. He had murdered many of our comrades and wanted the prisoners handed over to him. The lieutenant refused, said we were his prisoners and he would not hand them over. He had me sitting in the front seat of the truck. The major wanted him to take us to the Moncada but he did not hand us over to the major —there he saved our lives for the second time— nor did he take us to the Moncada. He took us to the precinct, in the middle of the city, saving my life for the third time. You see, and he was an officer of that army we were fighting against. When the Revolution triumphed, we promoted him to captain and he became aide to the first President of the country after the triumph.

As that lieutenant said, ideas cannot be killed (*applause*). Our ideas did not die, no one could kill them. And the ideas we sowed and developed during those thirty odd years until 1991 more or less, when the special period began, were what gave us the strength to resist. Without those years we had to educate, sow ideas, build awareness, instill feelings of solidarity and a generous internationalist spirit, our people would not have had the strength to resist.

I am speaking of things that are somewhat related to matters of political strategy. Very complicated things because they can be interpreted in different ways, and I know very well what I want to express. I have said that not even a Revolution like ours, which triumphed with the support of over 90% of the population, a unanimous, enthusiastic backing, great national unity, a tremendous political force, would have been able to resist. We would not have been able to preserve the Revolution under the current circumstances of the globalized world.

I do not advise anyone to stop fighting, one way or another. There are many ways, and among them the action of the masses, whose role and growing strength are always decisive.

Right now, we ourselves are involved in a great combat of ideas, disseminating our ideas all over, that is our job. It would not occur to us today to tell anyone: "Make a revolution like ours." Because under the circumstances that we think we know quite well, we would not be able to suggest: "Do what we did." Maybe if we were in those times we would say: "Do what we did." But in those times the world was different and the experience was different. Now we are more knowledgeable, more aware of the problems and, of course, respect and concern for others should come first and foremost.

At the time of the revolutionary movements in Central America, when the situation had become very difficult because the unipolar world already existed and not even the Nicaraguan revolution could stay in power, and peace negotiations were begun, we were visited quite often because of the long friendship relations existing with Cuba, and we were asked our views. We would tell them: "Do not ask our views about that. If we were in your place, we would know what to do, or we might be able to think what we should do. But you cannot give opinions to others when they are the ones who will have to apply opinions or criteria on matters as vital as fighting until death or negotiating. That decision only the revolutionaries of each country themselves can take. We will support whatever decision you make."

It was a unique experience, which I am telling in public for the first time too. Everyone has his own options but no one has the right to convey to others his own philosophy on facing life or death. That is why I say that giving opinions is a very delicate matter.

This does not hold true for criteria, viewpoints and opinions about global issues that affect the planet, recommendable tactics and strategies of struggle. As citizens of the world and part of the human race, we have the right to clearly express our thoughts to those who want to hear, be they revolutionaries or not.

We learned a long time ago how our relations with the progressive and revolutionary forces must be. Here, before you, I limit myself to conveying ideas, reflections, concepts in keeping with our common condition of Latin American patriots because, I repeat, I see a new hour in Venezuela, an immovable and inseparable pillar of the history of our America. One has the right to trust one's own experience or viewpoint. Not because one is infallible or because one has not made mistakes but because one has had the opportunity to take a 40 yearlong course in the academy of the Revolution.

That is why I have told you that you do not have a catastrophic situation, but you do have a difficult economic situation which entails risks for that opportunity that is looming.

There have been very impressive coincidences. This situation in Venezuela has taken place at a critical moment in the integration of Latin America; a special moment in which those further to the South, in their endeavor for unity, need help from those in northern South America (*applause*). In other words, they need your help. This has come at a moment in which the Caribbean countries need you. It has come at a moment when you can be the link, the bridge, the hinge whatever you want to call it, or a steel bridge between the Caribbean, Central America and South America.

Nobody like you is in a position to struggle for something so important and of so much priority at this difficult moment, as unity and integration, we might say, for the survival not only of Venezuela but of all the countries sharing our culture, our language and our race (*applause*).

Today more than ever we must be followers of Bolívar. Now more than ever we must raise the banner with the concept that humanity is our motherland, aware that we can only be saved if humanity is saved (*applause*). We can only be free —and we are very far from being free— if and when humanity is free. If and when we achieve a really fair world, which is possible and probable, although from so much observing, meditating and reading, I have reached the conclusion that humanity has very little time left to achieve this.

This is not only my opinion but the opinion of many other people I know. We recently held a Congress with 1000 economists, 600 of them from different foreign countries, many eminent people, and we discussed the papers presented. Fifty-five papers were discussed and debated concerning these problems of the neo-liberal globalization, the international economic crisis, things that are happening. Because I should have added that, unfortunately, I am not much hopeful that the prices of your commodities will increase in the next two or three years.

Our nickel has also declined by half its price. You see, not so long ago it was 8000 USD a ton, and now it is 4000 USD. Two days ago, sugar was six and a half cents, a price that does not even cover production costs; the cost of fuel, spare parts, labor force, productive inputs and so on. That is a social, and not only an economic problem. Hundreds of thousands of workers live by the sugar mills and are very much attached to them with deeply rooted traditions of sugar production, traditions that have been transmitted from generation to generation. And we are not going to close their factories although, right now, we are facing losses in sugar production.

We have some resources. Tourism, developed mainly with our own resources, has gained momentum in these years and we have made several decisions that have proved effective. I am not going to explain how we have managed to achieve what I have already explained. But I should say that we did it avoiding shock policies, the famous therapies that have been so insensitively applied elsewhere.

What we applied were austerity measures consulted with all the people. Before submitting such measures to Parliament, they were submitted to the people and discussed with all the trade unions, the workers and the peasants. We discussed what to do with the price of a given item, what price to increase and why, what price not to increase and why. That was also discussed with all the students in hundreds of thousands of assemblies. Then the measures were submitted to the National Assembly and later they were taken back to the grassroots again. Every decision was previously discussed because nothing is implemented unless there is a consensus and that is something that cannot be achieved by force.

The wise men in the North believe or pretend to believe that the Cuban Revolution is forcibly sustained. They have not been clever enough to realize that in our country, a country educated in high revolutionary and humane concepts that would be absolutely impossible (*laughter and applause*). This is only achieved through consensus and nothing else; no one in the world can make it if it is not with the people's massive support and cooperation. But consensus has its own rules. We learned to create it, to maintain it and to defend it. A united people ready to fight and win can be tremendously strong. Once there was a small disturbance that was not essentially political. It was a moment when the United States was encouraging through every means illegal exits to its territory. Cubans received automatic residence rights, something the US does not grant to citizens of any other country in the world. This was an encouragement for anyone to make a raft stronger than the Kon-Tiki or to use a motor boat to travel to that rich country assisted by the Gulf stream. Many people have sport vessels. Others stole boats and were welcomed as heroes, with all honors.

In an incident related to a plan to steal a passenger boat in the port of Havana to create a migratory disorder there was some turmoil and some began to throw stones against some store windows. What did we do then? We have never used soldiers or policemen against civilians. We have never had a fire engine throwing powerful jets of water against people, as one can see in those images from Europe itself almost every day, nor people wearing masks as if ready for a trip to outer space (*laughter and applause*). No, it is consensus that maintains and gives the Revolution its force.

That day I remember I was just getting to my office, it was about midday and I heard the news. I called my escorts, who were carrying weapons, and told them: "We are heading for the disturbances. You are forbidden to use your weapons!" I really preferred to have someone shoot at me than using weapons in this type of situation, that is why I gave them categorical instructions and they dutifully went there with me.

How long did the disturbances last? Minutes, seconds perhaps. Most of the people were perched in their balconies. They were somewhat shocked, surprised. Some underclass were throwing stones. And, suddenly, I think even those who were throwing stones started to applaud then the whole crowd moved and it was really impressive to see how the people react when it becomes aware of something that might harm the Revolution!

Well, I intended to get to the Havana City Museum where the city historian was. "How might Leal be?" He was said to be besieged in the Museum. But some blocks away, near the sea wall a whole crowd was walking with us and there were no signs of violence. I had said: "Not one unit should be moved, not one weapon, not one soldier." If you trust the people and if you have the trust of that people, you do not have to use weapons ever. We have never used them in our country (*applause*).

So what you need is unity, political culture and the conscious and militant support of the people. We built that through a long work. You, Venezuelans, will not be able to create it in a few days, nor in a few months.

If instead of being an old friend, someone to whom you have made the great honor of receiving with affection and trust, if instead of being an old and modest friend —I say it candidly, since I am totally convinced of it— if it were one of the Venezuelan forefathers who was here; I dare say more, if it were that great and talented man who dreamed of the unity of Latin America who was here, talking to you right now, he would say: "Save this process! Save this opportunity!" (*Prolonged applause.*)

I think you can be happy, and you will be happy, with many of the things you can do. Many already are at hand reach and depend on subjective factors and on very little resources. We have done that but one cannot realistically think of abundant resources: with some adding and subtracting it would be easy to understand. Yes, you can find resources, and you can find them in many things to meet priority, fundamental, essential requirements. But you cannot dream that the Venezuelan society will now have the resources it once had, under very different circumstances. The world is in crisis, prices for raw materials are very low, and the enemy would try to make use of that.

Rest assured that our neighbors on the North are not at all happy with the process that is taking place in Venezuela (*applause*), nor do they want it to succeed (*someone from the audience says something*).

I am not here to sow discord, quite the opposite. I would recommend wisdom and caution, all the necessary caution, and no more than necessary. But you have to be skilled politicians. You will even need to be skilled diplomats. You should avoid frightening many people. Based on my own experience of many years, not on my own intelligence, I suggest that you subtract as few people as possible (*laughter and applause*).

A transformation, a change, a revolution in the sense that word has today, when you look farther than the piece of land where you were born, when you think of the world, when you think of mankind, require the participation of the people. Better add than subtract. Look, that lieutenant who commanded the platoon that took me prisoner was added to our cause, not subtracted from it (*applause*). I took that man the way he was, and I have met some like him in my life. I would say I have met many like him.

It is true that the social environment, the social situation is the main factor in forging man's conscience. After all, I was the son of a landowner who had quite an extension of land in a country the size of Cuba, perhaps not so in Venezuela. My father had about 1000 hectares of land of his own and 10 000 hectares of leased land that he exploited. He was born in Spain and as a young and poor peasant was enrolled to fight against the Cubans.

Recently, in an important American magazine someone trying to offend the Spaniards, annoyed because the Spaniards have increased their investments in Latin America, published a very harsh article against Spain. One could see from that article that they were really angry. They want everything for themselves. They do not want a Spanish *peseta* invested in these lands, let alone in Cuba, and among other things the article said that in spite of his attacks against imperialism, Fidel Castro admires the re-conquest. The article construed things as if it were a Spanish re-conquest. It was entitled "In Search of the new El Dorado" and at one point in its furious attack it added that the Cuban ruler, the son of a Spanish soldier who fought on the wrong side during the war of independence, does not criticize the re-conquest.

I think about my father, who perhaps was 16 or 17 when he was enrolled over there and sent to Cuba as things were done in those days, and stationed in a Spanish fortified line. Could my father be really accused of fighting on the wrong side? No. In any case, he fought on the right side, he fought with the Spaniards. What do they want? That he should be an expert on Marxism, internationalism and a host of other things when he could barely read and write? (*Applause.*) I thought that they enlisted him and he fought on the right side. Those in the Yankee magazine are wrong. If he had fought on the Cuban side he would have been on the wrong side because this was not his country. He knew nothing about it. He could not even understand what the Cubans were fighting for. He was a conscript. He was brought here as they brought other hundreds of thousands of people. When the war ended, he was repatriated to Spain and he came back to Cuba a little after to work as a farmhand.

Later he became a landowner. I was born and I lived in a large state and it did not do me any harm. There I had my first friends. They were poor children of the place, the children of waged workers and modest peasants, victims all of the capitalist system. Later I went to schools that were more for the elite, but I came out unscathed, luckily. I really mean luckily. I had the fortune of being the son, and not the grandson of a landowner. If had I been the grandson of a landowner I would have probably been born and brought up in a city, among rich children, in a very high class neighborhood, and I would have never had my utopian or Marxist communist ideas nor anything similar.

No one is born a revolutionary, nor a poet or a warrior. It is the circumstances that make an individual or give him the opportunity of being one thing or the other.

If Columbus had been born a century before, no one would have heard of him. Spain was still under Arab occupation. If he had not been wrong and there had really been a path directly to China by sea without an unforeseen continent in between, he would have lasted 15 minutes on the coast of China. Remember that the Spaniards conquered Cuba with just twelve horses and in those days the Mongols already had cavalries with hundreds of thousands of soldiers (*applause*). See how things come to be.

I will not say anything about Bolívar, because he was born where he should, the day he should and in the way he should, that's it! (*applause*). I leave aside the scenario of what would have happened if he had been born a hundred years before or a hundred years later because that was impossible. (*Laughter.*) (*Cries from the audience: "Che!"*)

Che? Che [Guevara] has been present here every second, in my words, speaking from here (*prolonged applause*).

Now I will really finish. Some businessmen are waiting for me (*laughter*). How do I change my discourse? Well, I will tell them the same thing, honesty above all else (*laughter*). I believe that in this country there is a place for every honest person, for every sensitive person, for every person who can listen to the message of the homeland and of the times. I would say, the message of mankind is the one you should convey to your fellow countrymen and women.

I already told you about a meeting attended by 600 economists from various countries, many very intelligent people from the most diverse schools. We analyzed all these problems in depth. We did not want a sectarian, leftist or rightist meeting. We even invited Mr. Friedman but, of course, since he is now 82 he excused himself and said he could not come. We also invited Mr. Soros to defend his points of view; the Chicago Boys; the supply side monetarists; the neo-liberals, because what we wanted was to discuss, and we discussed for five days beginning on a Monday and concluding on a Friday.

That meeting was the result of a suggestion I had made at a meeting of Latin American economists. Many things were being said so I told them that with all the problems we are facing now, why could we not focus on the economic crisis and the problems of neo-liberal globalization? And so we did. Hundreds of papers were sent and 55 of them were chosen and all of them discussed. The others will be printed, the ones that were not discussed. They were very interesting, very educational and instructive. We were thinking of doing it every year. There is a forum in Davos, where I do not know how many representatives of transnationals and all the rich people in this world meet. Our small island can be a modest place where those who have no transnationals or anything of the sort can meet. But we are going to hold this meeting every year, based on the experience we had this time.

I had to close that meeting which lasted for five days. We had said: "Look, there will be no guitars to start the meeting." Because, as you know, meetings often start with guitars, with choruses...

Well, we had a chorus here, very well, a very good one (*laughter*). But I said: "The meeting is to begin exactly on time to discuss the first paper." And we did that for five days: morning, afternoon and evening sessions.

I had the task of closing the meeting and it was already midnight when I started talking. If you allow me, and it will only take some minutes, since it was very brief (*laughter*). I would like to repeat today what I said, because it covers very concisely the essence of many of the things I have said here.

"Esteemed delegates, observers and guests,

"You have honored me by asking but I will not make a speech. I will limit myself to presenting a paper. I will do it in the style of a cablegram and it will mostly be a dialogue with myself.

"Month of July. Latin American and Caribbean Economists Meeting. Subject:

Serious world economic crisis in sight. Need to convene an international conference. Focal point: Economic crisis and neo-liberal globalization.

"Extensive debate.

"Every school of thought represented.

"Exchange of arguments.

"Work done along these lines.

"Maximum possible reduction of expenses for everyone.

"Morning, afternoon and evening sessions.

"Exceptional seriousness and discipline have prevailed during these five days.

"We have all expressed ourselves in absolute freedom. We have made it. We are grateful.

"We have learned a lot from listening to you.

"A great variety and diversity of ideas. An extraordinary show of scholarly spirit and talent clearly and beautifully expressed.

"We all have our convictions.

"We can all influence each other.

"In the long run, we shall all reach similar conclusions.

"My deepest convictions: the incredible and unprecedented globalization under discussion is a product of historical evolution, a fruit of human civilization achieved in a very short period of time, in no more than 3000 years of the long presence of our ancestors on the planet. They were already a completely developed specie. The man of today is not more intelligent than Pericle, Plato or Aristotle, and we do not know as yet if he is intelligent enough to solve today's extremely complex problems. We are betting on his doing it. That is what we have dealt with at our meeting.

"A question: Is it a reversible process? My answer, the one I give to myself, is No.

"What kind of globalization have we today? A neo-liberal globalization, that is what many of us call it. Is it sustainable? No. Will it be able to subsist for long? Absolutely, no. Is it a matter of centuries? Categorically, no. Will it last only decades? Yes, only decades. But rather sooner than later it will cease to exist.

"Do I believe myself to be a sort of prophet of fortune-teller? No. Do I know much about economics? No. Hardly anything. To make this statement it is enough to know how to add up, subtract, multiply and divide something children learn in grammar school.

"How will such transition take place? We do not know. Will it be through violent revolutions or devastating wars? That seems unlikely, irrational and suicidal. Will it be through deep and catastrophic crises? Unfortunately, this is most likely, almost inevitable and it will happen through many different ways and forms of struggle.

"What kind of globalization will it be? It cannot but be supportive, socialist, communist or whatever you want to call it.

"Does nature, and the human species with it, have much time left to survive in the absence of such change? Very little time. Who will be the builders of that new world? The men and women who inhabit our planet.

"Which will be their basic weapons? Ideas will be, and consciousness. Who will sow them, cultivate them and make them invincible? You will. Is it a utopia, just one more dream among so many others? No, because it is objectively inevitable and there is no alternative to it. It has been dreamed of before, only perhaps too early. As the most visionary of the sons and daughters of this island, José Martí, said: 'Today's dreams will be tomorrow's realities.'

"I have concluded my presentation. Thank you." (*Ovation.*)

I am sorry I have been so imposing and I promise you that in forty years, when you invite me again, I will be more concise. (*Applause and exclamations: "Fidel! Fidel! Fidel!"*)

You were lucky I did not include the famous booklet. You know what it was? The paper on the Synod in Rome, published in mexico (*someone in the audience says something*). I was not going to read it, but much of what I underlined when reading this apostolic exhortation coincided with many of the ideas I expressed here. I was going to use it as an evidence that much of what is being thought today in the world on the calamitous existing system does not only come from leftist sources, not only comes from political sources. Arguments, expressions or contentions condemning poverty, injustices, inequalities, neo-liberalism, the squandering of consumer societies and many other social and human disasters resulting from the present economic order imposed on the world also come from institutions that cannot be suspected of Marxism, such as the Roman Catholic Church. Many other Christian churches think likewise.

Perhaps it would have been best to come with this paper and read what I had underlined. That way you would have been able to leave four hours and a half earlier (*laughter*).

Thank you, very much.
(*Ovation.*)